THE GHOST-SEER (OR THE APPARITIONIST), AND SPORT OF DESTINY

FREDERICH SCHILLER

FROM THE PAPERS OF COUNT O

I am about to relate an adventure which to many will appear incredible, but of which I was in great part an eye-witness. The few who are acquainted with a certain political event will, if indeed these pages should happen to find them alive, receive a welcome solution thereof. And, even to the rest of my readers, it will be, perhaps, important as a contribution to the history of the deception and aberrations of the human intellect. The boldness of the schemes which malice is able to contemplate and to carry out must excite astonishment, as must also the means of which it can avail itself to accomplish its aims. Clear, unvarnished truth shall guide my pen; for, when these pages come before the public, I shall be no more, and shall therefore never learn their fate.

On my return to Courland in the year 17--, about the time of the Carnival, I visited the Prince of ------- at Venice. We had been acquainted in the ------ service, and we here renewed an intimacy which, by the restoration of peace, had been interrupted. As I wished to see the curiosities of this city, and as the prince was waiting only for the arrival of remittances to return to his native country, he easily prevailed on me to tarry till his departure. We agreed not to separate during the time of our residence at Venice, and the prince was kind enough to accommodate me at his lodgings at the Moor Hotel.

As the prince wished to enjoy himself, and his small revenues did not permit him to maintain the dignity of his rank, he lived at Venice in the strictest incognito. Two noblemen, in whom he had entire confidence, and a few faithful servants, composed all his retinue. He shunned expenditure, more however from inclination than economy. He avoided all kinds of dissipation, and up to the age of thirty-five years had resisted the numerous allurements of this voluptuous city. To the charms of the fair sex he was wholly indifferent. A settled gravity and an enthusiastic melancholy were the prominent features of his character. His affections were tranquil, but obstinate to excess. He formed his attachments with caution and timidity, but when once formed they were cordial and permanent. In the midst of a tumultuous crowd he walked in solitude. Wrapped in his own visionary ideas, he was often a stranger to the world about him; and, sensible of his own deficiency in the knowledge of mankind, he scarcely ever ventured an opinion of his own, and was apt to pay an unwarrantable deference to the judgment of others. Though far from being weak, no man was more liable to be governed; but, when conviction had once entered his mind, he became firm and decisive; equally courageous to combat an acknowledged prejudice or to die for a new one.

As he was the third prince of his house, he had no likely prospect of succeeding to the sovereignty. His ambition had never been awakened; his passions had taken another direction. Contented to find himself independent of the will of others, he never enforced his own as a law; his utmost wishes did not soar beyond the peaceful quietude of a private life, free from care. He read much, but without discrimination. As his education had been neglected, and, as he had early entered the career of arms, his understanding had never been fully matured. Hence the knowledge he afterwards acquired served but to increase the chaos of his ideas, because it was built on an unstable foundation.

He was a Protestant, as all his family had been, by birth, but not by investigation, which he had never attempted, although at one period of his life he had been an enthusiast in its cause. He had never, so far as came to my knowledge, been a freemason.

One evening we were, as usual, walking by ourselves, well masked in the square of St. Mark. It was growing late, and the crowd was dispersing, when the prince observed a mask which followed us everywhere. This mask was an Armenian, and walked alone. We quickened our steps, and endeavored to baffle him by repeatedly altering our course. It was in vain, the mask was always close behind us. "You have had no intrigue here, I hope," said the prince at last, "the husbands of Venice are dangerous." "I do not know a single lady in the place," was my answer. "Let us sit down here, and speak German," said he; "I fancy we are mistaken for some other persons." We sat down upon a stone bench, and expected the mask would have passed by. He came directly up to us, and took his seat by the side of the prince. The latter took out his watch, and, rising at the same time, addressed me thus in a loud voice in French, "It is past nine. Come, we forget that we are waited for at the Louvre." This speech he only invented in order to deceive the mask as to our route. "Nine!" repeated the latter in the same language, in a slow and expressive voice, "Congratulate yourself, my prince" (calling him by his real name); "he died at nine." In saying this, he rose and went away.

We looked at each other in amazement. "Who is dead?" said the prince at length, after a long silence. "Let us follow him," replied I, "and demand an explanation." We searched every corner of the place; the mask was nowhere to be found. We returned to our hotel disappointed. The prince spoke not a word to me the whole way; he walked apart by himself, and appeared to be greatly agitated, which he afterwards confessed to me was the case. Having reached home, he began at length to speak: "Is it not laughable," said he, "that a madman should have the power thus to disturb a man's tranquillity by two or three words?" We wished each other a goodnight; and, as soon as I was in my own apartment, I noted down in my pocket-book the day and the hour when this adventure happened. It was on a Thursday.

The next evening the prince said to me, "Suppose we go to the square of St. Mark, and seek for our mysterious Armenian. I long to see this comedy unravelled." I consented. We walked in the square till eleven. The Armenian was nowhere to be seen. We repeated our walk the four following evenings, and each time with the same bad success.

On the sixth evening, as we went out of the hotel, it occurred to me, whether designedly or otherwise I cannot recollect, to tell the servants where we might be found in case we should be inquired for. The prince remarked my precaution, and approved of it with a smile. We found the square of St. Mark very much crowded. Scarcely had we advanced thirty steps when I perceived the Armenian, who was pressing rapidly through the crowd, and seemed to be in search of some one. We were just approaching him, when Baron F-----, one of the prince's retinue, came up to us quite breathless, and delivered to the prince a letter. "It is sealed with black," said he, "and we supposed from this that it might contain matters of importance." I was struck as with a thunderbolt. The prince went near a torch, and began to read. "My cousin is dead!" exclaimed he. "When?" inquired I anxiously, interrupting him. He looked again into the letter. "Last Thursday night at nine."

We had not recovered from our surprise when the Armenian stood before us. "You are known here, my prince!" said he. "Hasten to your hotel. You will find there the deputies from the Senate. Do not hesitate to accept the honor they intend to offer you. Baron I--forgot to tell you that your remittances are arrived." He disappeared among the crowd.

We hastened to our hotel, and found everything as the Armenian had told us. Three noblemen of the republic were waiting to pay their respects to the prince, and to escort him in state to the Assembly, where the first nobility of the city were ready to receive him. He had hardly time enough to give me a hint to sit up for him till his return.

About eleven o'clock at night he returned. On entering the room he appeared grave and thoughtful. Having dismissed the servants, he took me by the hand, and said, in the words of Hamlet, "Count -----

"'There are more things in heav'n and earth, Than are dreamt of in your philosophy.'"

"Gracious prince!" replied I, "you seem to forget that you are retiring to your pillow greatly enriched in prospect." The deceased was the hereditary prince.

"Do not remind me of it," said the prince; "for should I even have acquired a crown I am now too much engaged to occupy myself with such a trifle. If that Armenian has not merely guessed by chance--"

"How can that be, my prince?" interrupted I.

"Then will I resign to you all my hopes of royalty in exchange for a monk's cowl."

I have mentioned this purposely to show how far every ambitious idea was then distant from his thoughts.

The following evening we went earlier than usual to the square of St. Mark. A sudden shower of rain obliged us to take shelter in a coffee-house, where we found a party engaged at cards. The prince took his place behind the chair of a Spaniard to observe the game. I went into an adjacent chamber to read the newspapers. A short time afterwards I heard a noise in the card-room. Previously to the entrance of the prince the Spaniard had been constantly losing, but since then he had won upon every card. The fortune of the game was reversed in a striking manner, and the bank was in danger of being challenged by the pointeur, whom this lucky change of fortune had rendered more adventurous. A Venetian, who kept the bank, told the prince in a very rude manner that his presence interrupted the fortune of the game, and desired him to quit the table. The latter looked coldly at him, remained in his place, and preserved the same countenance, when the Venetian repeated his insulting demand in French. He thought the prince understood neither French nor Italian; and, addressing himself with a contemptuous laugh to the company, said "Pray, gentlemen, tell me how I must make myself understood to this fool." At the same time he rose and prepared to seize the prince by the arm. His patience forsook the latter; he grasped the Venetian with a strong hand, and threw him violently on the ground. The company rose up in confusion. Hearing the noise, I hastily entered the room, and unguardedly called the prince by his name. "Take care," said I, imprudently; "we are in Venice." The name of the prince caused a general silence, which ended in a whispering which appeared to me to have a dangerous tendency. All the Italians present divided into parties, and kept aloof. One after the other left the room, so that we soon found ourselves alone with the Spaniard and a few Frenchmen. "You are lost, prince," said they, "if you do not leave the city immediately. The Venetian whom you have handled so roughly is rich enough to hire a bravo. It costs him but fifty zechins to be revenged by your death." The Spaniard offered, for the security of the prince, to go for the guards, and even to accompany us home himself. The Frenchmen proposed to do the same. We were still deliberating what to do when the doors suddenly opened, and some officers of the Inquisition entered the room. They produced an order of government, which charged us both to follow them immediately. They conducted us under a strong escort to the canal, where a gondola was waiting for us, in which we were ordered to embark. We were blindfolded before we landed. They led us up a large stone staircase, and through a long, winding passage, over vaults, as I judged from the echoes that resounded under our feet. At length we came to another staircase, and, having descended a flight of steps, we entered a hall, where the bandage was removed from our eyes.

We found ourselves in a circle of venerable old men, all dressed in black; the hall was hung round with black and dimly lighted. A dead silence reigned in the assembly, which inspired us with a feeling of awe. One of the old men, who appeared to be the principal Inquisitor, approached the prince with a solemn countenance, and said, pointing to the Venetian, who was led forward:

"Do you recognize this man as the same who offended you at the coffee-house?"

"I do," answered the prince.

Then addressing the prisoner: "Is this the same person whom you meant to have assassinated to-night?"

The prisoner replied, "Yes."

In the same instant the circle opened, and we saw with horror the head of the Venetian severed from his body.

"Are you content with this satisfaction?" said the Inquisitor. The prince had fainted in the arms of his attendants. "Go," added the Inquisitor, turning to me, with a terrible voice, "Go; and in future judge less hastily of the administration of justice in Venice."

Who the unknown friend was who had thus saved us from inevitable death, by interposing in our behalf the active arm of justice, we could not conjecture. Filled with terror we reached our hotel. It was past midnight.

The chamberlain, Z-------, was waiting anxiously for us at the door.

"How fortunate it was that you sent us a message," said he to the prince, as he lighted us up the staircase. "The news which Baron F----- soon after brought us respecting you from the square of St. Mark would otherwise have given us the greatest uneasiness."

"I sent you a message!" said the prince. "When? I know nothing of it."

"This evening, after eight, you sent us word that we must not be alarmed if you should come home later to-night than usual."

The prince looked at me. "Perhaps you have taken this precaution without mentioning it to me."

I knew nothing of it.

"It must be so, however," replied the chamberlain, "since here is your repeating-watch, which you sent me as a mark of authenticity."

The prince put his hand to his watch-pocket. It was empty, and he recognized the watch which the chamberlain held as his own.

"Who brought it?" said he, in amazement.

"An unknown mask, in an Armenian dress, who disappeared immediately."

We stood looking at each other. "What do you think of this?" said the prince at last, after a long silence. "I have a secret guardian here in Venice."

The frightful transaction of this night threw the prince into a fever, which confined him to his room for a week. During this time our hotel was crowded with Venetians and strangers, who visited the prince from a deference to his newly-discovered rank. They vied with each other in offers of service, and it was not a little entertaining to observe that the last visitor seldom failed to hint some suspicion derogatory to the character of the preceding one. Billets-doux and nostrums poured in upon us from all quarters. Every one endeavored to recommend himself in his own way. Our adventure with the Inquisition was no more mentioned. The court of, wishing the prince to delay his departure from Venice for some time, orders were sent to several bankers to pay him considerable sums of money. He was thus, against his will, compelled to protract his residence in Italy; and at his request I also resolved to postpone my departure for some time longer.

As soon as the prince had recovered strength enough to quit his chamber he was advised by his physician to take an airing in a gondola upon the Brenta, for the benefit of the air, to which, as the weather was serene, he readily consented. Just as the prince was about to step into the boat he missed the key of a little chest in which some very valuable papers were enclosed.. We immediately turned back to search for it. He very distinctly remembered that he had locked the chest the day before, and he had never left the room in the interval. As our endeavors to find it proved ineffectual, we were obliged to relinquish the search in order to avoid being too late. The prince, whose soul was above suspicion, gave up the key as lost, and desired that it might not be mentioned any more.

Our little voyage was exceedingly delightful. A picturesque country, which at every winding of the river seemed to increase in richness and beauty; the serenity of the sky, which formed a May day in the middle of February; the charming gardens and elegant countryseats which adorned the banks of the Brenta; the maestic city of Venice behind us, with its lofty spires, and a forest of masts, rising as it were out of the waves; all this afforded us one of the most splendid prospects in the world. We wholly abandoned ourselves to the enchantment of Nature's luxuriant scenery; our minds shared the hilarity of the day; even the prince himself lost his wonted gravity, and vied with us in merry jests and diversions. On landing about two Italian miles from the city we heard the sound of sprightly music; it came from a small village at a little distance from the Brenta, where there was at that time a fair. The place was crowded with company of every description. A troop of young girls and boys, dressed in theatrical habits, welcomed us in a pantomimical dance. The invention was novel; animation and grace attended their every movement. Before the dance was quite concluded the principal actress, who represented a queen, stopped suddenly, as if arrested by an invisible arm. Herself and those around her were motionless. The music ceased. The assembly was silent. Not a breath was to be heard, and the queen stood with her eyes fixed on the ground in deep abstraction. On a sudden she started from her reverie with the fury of one inspired, and looked wildly around her. "A king is among us," she exclaimed, taking her crown from her head, and laying it at the feet of the prince. Every one present cast their eyes upon him, and doubted for some time whether there was any meaning in this farce; so much were they deceived by the impressive seriousness of the actress. This silence was at length broken by a general clapping of hands, as a mark of approbation. I looked at the prince. I noticed that he appeared not a little disconcerted, and endeavored to escape the inquisitive glances of the spectators. He threw money to the players, and hastened to extricate himself from the crowd.

We had advanced but a few steps when a venerable barefooted friar, pressing through the crowd, placed himself in the prince's path. "My lord," said he, "give the holy Virgin part of your gold. You will want her prayers." He uttered these words in a tone of voice which startled us extremely, and then disappeared in the throng.

In the meantime our company had increased. An English lord, whom the prince had seen before at Nice, some merchants of Leghorn, a German prebendary, a French abbe with some ladies, and a Russian officer, attached themselves to our party. The physiognomy of the latter had something so uncommon as to attract our particular attention. Never in my life did I see such various features and so little expression; so much attractive benevolence and such forbidding coldness in the same face. Each passion seemed by turns to have exercised its ravages on it, and to have successively abandoned it. Nothing remained but the calm, piercing look of a person deeply skilled in the knowledge of mankind; but it was a look that abashed every one on whom it was directed. This extraordinary man followed us at a distance, and seemed apparently to take but little interest in what was passing.

We came to a booth where there was a lottery. The ladies bought shares. We followed their example, and the prince himself purchased a ticket. He won a snuffbox. As he opened it I saw him turn pale and start back. It contained his lost key.

"How is this?" said he to me, as we were left for a moment alone. "A superior power attends me, omniscience surrounds me. An invisible being, whom I cannot escape, watches over my steps. I must seek for the Armenian, and obtain an explanation from him."

The sun was setting when we arrived at the pleasurehouse, where a supper had been prepared for us. The prince's name had augmented our company to sixteen. Besides the above-mentioned persons there was a virtuoso from Rome, several Swiss gentlemen, and an adventurer from Palermo in regimentals, who gave himself out for a captain. We resolved to spend the evening where we were, and to return home by torchlight. The conversation at table was lively. The prince could not forbear relating his adventure of the key, which excited general astonishment. A warm dispute on the subject presently took place. Most of the company positively maintained that the pretended occult sciences were nothing better than juggling tricks. The French abbe, who had drank rather too much wine, challenged the whole tribe of ghosts, the English lord uttered blasphemies, and the musician made a cross to exorcise the devil. Some few of the company, amongst whom was the prince, contended that opinions respecting such matters ought to be kept to oneself. In the meantime the Russian officer discoursed with the ladies, and did not seem to pay attention to any part of conversation. In the heat of the dispute no one observed that the Sicilian had left the room. In less than half an hour he returned wrapped in a cloak, and placed himself behind the chair of the Frenchman. "A few moments ago," said he, "you had the temerity to challenge the whole tribe of ghosts. Would you wish to make a trial with one of them?"

"I will," answered the abbe, "if you will take upon yourself to introduce one."

"That I am ready to do," replied the Sicilian, turning to us, "as soon as these ladies and gentlemen have left us."

"Why only then?" exclaimed the Englishman. "A courageous ghost will surely not be afraid of a cheerful company."

"I would not answer for the consequences," said the Sicilian.

"For heaven's sake, no!" cried the ladies, starting affrighted from their chairs.

"Call your ghost," said the abbe, in a tone of defiance, "but warn him beforehand that there are sharp-pointed weapons here." At the same time he asked one of the company for a sword.

"If you preserve the same intention in his presence," answered the Sicilian, coolly, "you may then act as you please." He then turned towards the prince: "Your highness," said he, "asserts that your key has been in the hands of a stranger; can you conjecture in whose?"

"No"

"Have you no suspicion?"

"It certainly occurred to me that"--

"Should you know the person if you saw him?" "Undoubtedly."

The Sicilian, throwing back his cloak, took out a looking-glass and held it before the prince. "Is this the man?"

The prince drew back with affright. "Whom have you seen?" I inquired. "The Armenian."

The Sicilian concealed his looking-glass under his cloak.

"Is it the person whom you thought of?" demanded the whole company. "The same."

A sudden change manifested itself on every face; no more laughter was to be heard. All eyes were fixed with curiosity on the Sicilian.

"Monsieur l'Abbe! The matter grows serious," said the Englishman. "I advise you to think of beating a retreat."

"The fellow is in league with the devil," exclaimed the Frenchman, and rushed out of the house. The ladies ran shrieking from the room. The virtuoso followed them. The German prebendary was snoring in a chair. The Russian officer continued sitting in his place as before, perfectly indifferent to what was passing.

"Perhaps your attention was only to raise a laugh at the expense of that boaster," said the prince, after they were gone, "or would you indeed fulfil your promise to us?"

"It is true," replied the Sicilian; "I was but jesting with the abbe. I took him at his word, because I knew very well that the coward would not suffer me

11

to proceed to extremities. The matter itself is, however, too serious to serve merely as a jest."

"You grant, then, that it is in your power?"

The sorcerer maintained a long silence, and kept his look fixed steadily on the prince, as if to examine him.

"It is!" answered he at last.

The prince's curiosity was now raised to the highest pitch. A fondness for the marvellous had ever been his prevailing weakness. His improved understanding and a proper course of reading had for some time dissipated every idea of this kind; but the appearance of the Armenian had revived them. He stepped aside with the Sicilian, and I heard them in very earnest conversation.

"You see in me," said the prince, "a man who burns with impatience to be convinced on this momentous subject. I would embrace as a benefactor, I would cherish as my best friend him who could dissipate my doubts and remove the veil from my eyes. Would you render me this important service?"

"What is your request!" inquired the Sicilian, hesitating.

"For the present I only beg some proof of your art. Let me see an apparition."

"To what will this lead?"

"After a more intimate acquaintance with me you may be able to judge whether I deserve further instruction."

"I have the greatest esteem for your highness, gracious prince. A secret power in your countenance, of which you yourself are as yet ignorant, drew me at first sight irresistibly towards you. You are more powerful than you are yourself aware. You may command me to the utmost extent of my power, but--" "Then let me see an apparition."

"But I must first be certain that you do not require it from mere curiosity. Though the invisible powers are in some degree at my command, it is on the sacred condition that I do not abuse my authority."

"My intentions are most pure. I want truth."

They left their places, and removed to a distant window, where I could no longer hear them. The English lord, who had likewise overheard this conversation, took me aside. "Your prince has a noble mind. I am sorry for him. I will pledge my salvation that he has to do with a rascal."

"Everything depends on the manner in which the sorcerer will extricate himself from this business."

"Listen to me. The poor devil is now pretending to be scrupulous. He will not show his tricks unless he hears the sound of gold. There are nine of us. Let us make a collection. That will spoil his scheme, and perhaps open the eyes of the prince."

"I am content." The Englishman threw six guineas upon a plate, and went round gathering subscriptions. Each of us contributed some louis-d'ors. The Russian officer was particularly pleased with our proposal; he laid a bank-note of one hundred zechins on the plate, a piece of extravagance which startled the Englishman. We brought the collection to the prince. "Be so kind," said the English lord, "as to entreat this gentleman in our names to let us see a specimen of his art, and to accept of this small token of our gratitude." The prince added a ring of value, and offered the whole to the Sicilian. He hesitated a few moments. "Gentlemen," answered he, "I am humbled by this generosity, but I yield to your request. Your wishes shall be gratified." At the same time he rang the bell. "As for this money," continued he, "to which I have no right myself, permit me to send it to the next monastery to be applied to pious uses. I shall only keep this ring as a precious memorial of the worthiest of princes."

Here the landlord entered; and the Sicilian handed him over the money. "He is a rascal notwithstanding," whispered the Englishman to me. "He refuses the money because at present his designs are chiefly on the prince."

"Whom do you wish to see?" asked the sorcerer.

The prince considered for a moment. "We may as well have a great man at once," said the Englishman. "Ask for Pope Ganganelli. It can make no difference to this gentleman."

The Sicilian bit his lips. "I dare not call one of the Lord's anointed."

"That is a pity!" replied the English lord; "perhaps we might have heard from him what disorder he died of."

"The Marquis de Lanoy," began the prince, "was a French brigadier in the late war, and my most intimate friend. Having received a mortal wound in the battle of Hastinbeck, he was carried to my tent, where he soon after died in my arms. In his last agony he made a sign for me to approach. 'Prince,' said he to me, 'I shall never again behold my native land. I must, therefore, acquaint you with a secret known to none but myself. In a convent on the frontiers of Flanders lives a --------' He expired. Death cut short the thread of his discourse. I wish to see my friend to hear the remainder."

"You ask much," exclaimed the Englishman, with an oath. "I proclaim you the greatest sorcerer on earth if you can solve this problem," continued he, turning to the Sicilian. We admired the wise choice of the prince, and unanimously gave our approval to the proposition. In the meantime the sorcerer paced up and down the room with hasty steps, apparently struggling with himself.

"This was all that the dying marquis communicated to you?" "It is all."

"Did you make no further inquiries about the matter in his native country?" "I did, but they all proved fruitless."

"Had the Marquis de Lanoy led an irreproachable life? I dare not call up every shade indiscriminately."

"He died, repenting the excesses of his youth." "Do you carry with you any token of his!"

"I do." (The prince had really a snuff-box with the marquis' portrait enamelled in miniature on the lid, which he had placed upon the table near his plate during the time of supper.)

"I do not want to know what it is. If you will leave me you shall see the deceased."

He requested us to wait in the other pavilion until he should call us. At the same time he caused all the furniture to be removed from the room, the windows to be taken out, and the shutters to be bolted. He ordered the innkeeper, with whom he appeared to be intimately connected, to bring a vessel with burning coals, and carefully to extinguish every fire in the house. Previous to our leaving the room he obliged us separately to pledge our honor that we would maintain an everlasting silence respecting everything we should see and hear. All the doors of the pavilion we were in were bolted behind us when we left it.

It was past eleven, and a dead silence reigned throughout the whole house. As we were retiring from the saloon the Russian officer asked me whether we had loaded pistols. "For what purpose?" asked I. "They may possibly be of some use," replied he. "Wait a moment. I will provide some." He went away. The Baron F------ and I opened a window opposite the pavilion we had left. We fancied we heard two persons whispering to each other, and a noise like that of a ladder applied to one of the windows. This was, however, a mere conjecture, and I did not dare affirm it as a fact. The Russian officer came back with a brace of pistols, after having been absent about half an hour. We saw him load them with powder and ball. It was almost two o'clock in the morning when the sorcerer came and announced that all was prepared. Before we entered the room he desired us to take off our shoes, and to appear in our shirts, stockings, and under-garments. He bolted the doors after us as before.

We found in the middle of the room a large, black circle, drawn with charcoal, the space within which was capable of containing us all very easily. The planks of the chamber floor next to the wall were taken up all round the room, so that we stood as it were upon an island. An altar covered with black cloth was placed in the centre upon a carpet of red satin. A Chaldee Bible was laid open, together with a skull; and a silver crucifix was fastened upon the altar. Instead of candles some spirits of wine were burning in a silver vessel. A thick smoke of frankincense darkened the room and almost extinguished the lights. The sorcerer was undressed like ourselves, but barefooted; about his bare neck he wore an amulet, suspended by a chain of human hair; round his middle was a white apron marked with cabalistic characters and symbolical figures.

[Amulet is a charm or preservative against mischief, witchcraft, or diseases. Amulets were made of stone metal, simples, animals, and everything which fancy or caprice suggested; and sometimes they consisted of words, characters, and sentences ranged in a particular order and engraved upon wood, and worn about the neck or some other part of the body. At other times they were neither written nor engraved, but prepared with many superstitious ceremonies, great regard being usually paid to the influence of the stars. The Arabians have given to this species of amulets the name of talismans. All nations have been fond of amulets. The Jews were extremely superstitious in the use of them to drive away diseases; and even amongst the Christians of the early times amulets were made of the wood of the cross or ribbons, with a text of Scripture written on them, as preservatives against diseases.]

He desired us to join hands and to observe profound silence; above all he ordered us not to ask the apparition any question. He desired the Englishman and myself, whom he seemed to distrust the most, constantly to hold two naked swords crossways an inch above his head as long as the conjuration should last. We formed a half-moon round him; the Russian officer placed himself close to the English lord, and was the nearest to the altar. The sorcerer stood upon the satin carpet with his face turned to the east. He sprinkled holy water in the direction of the four cardinal points of the compass, and bowed three times before the Bible. The formula of the conjuration, of which we did not understand a word, lasted for the space of seven or eight minutes, at the end of which he made a sign to those who stood close behind to seize him firmly by the hair. Amid the most violent convulsions he called the deceased three times by his name, and the third time he stretched forth his hand towards the crucifix.

On a sudden we all felt at the same instant a stroke as of a flash of lightning, so powerful that it obliged us to quit each other's hands; a terrible thunder shook the house; the locks jarred; the doors creaked; the cover of the silver box fell down and extinguished the light; and on the opposite wall over the chimney-piece appeared a human figure in a bloody shirt, with the paleness of death on its countenance.

"Who calls me?" said a hollow, hardly intelligible voice.

"Thy friend," answered the sorcerer, "who respects thy memory, and prays for thy soul." He named the prince.

The answers of the apparition were always given at very long intervals. "What does he want with me?" continued the voice.

"He wants to hear the remainder of the confession which then had begun to impart to him in thy dying hour, but did not finish."

"In a convent on the frontiers of Flanders lives a -------"The house again trembled; a dreadful thunder rolled; a flash of lightning illuminated the room; the doors flew open, and another human figure, bloody and pale as the first, but more terrible, appeared on the threshold. The spirit in the box began to burn again by itself, and the hall was light as before.

"Who is amongst us?" exclaimed the sorcerer, terrified, casting a look of horror on the assemblage; "I did not want thee." The figure advanced with noiseless and majestic steps directly up to the altar, stood on the satin Carpet over against us, and touched the crucifix. The first apparition was seen no more.

"Who calls me?" demanded the second apparition.

"The sorcerer began to tremble. Terror and amazement kept us motionless for some time. I seized a pistol. The sorcerer snatched it out of my hand, and fired it at the apparition. The ball rolled slowly upon the altar, and the figure emerged unaltered from the smoke. The Sorcerer fell senseless on the ground.

"What is this?" exclaimed the Englishman, in astonishment, aiming a blow at the ghost with a sword. The figure touched his arm, and the weapon fell to the ground. The perspiration stood on my brow with horror. Baron ----- - afterwards confessed to me that he had prayed silently.

During all this time the prince stood fearless and tranquil, his eyes riveted on the second apparition. "Yes, I know thee," said he at length, with emotion; "thou art Lanoy; thou art my friend. Whence comest thou?"

"Eternity is mute. Ask me concerning my past life."

"Who is it that lives in the convent which thou mentionedst to me in thy last moments?"

"My daughter."

"How? Hast thou been a father?" "Woe is me that I was not."

"Art thou not happy, Lanoy?" "God has judged."

"Can I render thee any further service in this world?" "None but to think of thyself."

"How must I do that?" "Thou wilt learn at Rome."

The thunder again rolled; a black cloud of smoke filled the room; when it had dispersed the figure was no longer visible. I forced open one of the window shutters. It was daylight.

The sorcerer now recovered from his swoon. "Where are we?" asked he, seeing the daylight.

The Russian officer stood close beside him, and looked over his shoulder. "Juggler," said he to him, with a terrible countenance, "Thou shalt summon no more ghosts."

The Sicilian turned round, looked steadfastly in his face, uttered a loud shriek, and threw himself at his feet.

We looked all at once at the pretended Russian. The prince instantly recognized the features of the Armenian, and the words he was about to utter expired on his tongue. We were all as it were petrified with fear and amazement. Silent and motionless, our eyes were fixed on this mysterious being, who beheld us with a calm but penetrating look of grandeur and superiority. A minute elapsed in this awful silence; another succeeded; not a breath was to be heard.

A violent battering against the door roused us at last from this stupor. The door fell in pieces into the room, and several officers of justice, with a guard, rushed in. "Here they are, all together," said the leader to his followers. Then addressing himself to us, "In the name of the government," continued he, "I arrest you." We had no time to recollect ourselves; in a few moments we were surrounded. The Russian officer, whom I shall again call the Armenian, took the chief officer aside, and, as far as I in my confusion could notice, I observed him whisper a few words to the latter, and show him a written paper. The officer, bowing respectfully, immediately quitted him, turned to us, and taking off his hat, said "Gentlemen, I humbly beg your pardon for having confounded you with this impostor. I shall not inquire who you are, as this gentleman assures me you are men of honor." At the same time he gave his companions a sign to leave us at liberty. He ordered the Sicilian to be bound and strictly guarded. "The fellow is ripe for punishment," added he; "we have been searching for him these seven months."

[margin note: because of his sorcery?]

The wretched sorcerer was really an object of pity. The terror caused by the second apparition, and by this unexpected arrest, had together overpowered his senses. Helpless as a child, he suffered himself to be bound without resistance. His eyes were wide open and immovable; his face was pale as death; his lips quivered convulsively, but he was unable to utter a sound.

Every moment we expected he would fall into a fit. The prince was moved by the situation in which he saw him. He undertook to procure his discharge from the leader of the police, to whom he discovered his rank. "Do you know, gracious prince," said the officer, "for whom your highness is so generously interceding? The juggling tricks by which he endeavored to deceive you are the least of his crimes. We have secured his accomplices; they depose terrible facts against him. He may think himself fortunate if he is only punished with the galleys."

In the meantime we saw the innkeeper and his family led bound through the yard. "This man, too?" said the prince; "and what is his crime?"

"He was his comrade and accomplice," answered the officer. "He assisted him in his deceptions and robberies, and shared the booty with him. Your highness shall be convinced of it presently. Search the house," continued he, turning to his followers, "and bring me immediate notice of what you find."

The prince looked around for the Armenian, but he had disappeared. In the confusion occasioned by the arrival of the watch he had found means to steal away unperceived. The prince was inconsolable; he declared he would send all his servants, and would himself go in search of this mysterious man; and he wished me to go with him. I hastened to the window; the house was surrounded by a great number of idlers, whom the account of this event had attracted to the spot. It was impossible to get through the crowd. I represented this to the prince. "If," said I, "it is the Armenian's intention to conceal himself from us, he is doubtless better acquainted with the intricacies of the place than we, and all our inquiries would prove fruitless. Let us rather remain here a little longer, gracious prince," added I. "This officer, to whom, if I observed right, he discovered himself, may perhaps give us some information respecting him."

We now for the first time recollected that we were still undressed. We hastened to the other pavilion and put on our clothes as quickly as possible. When we returned they had finished searching the house.

On removing the altar and some of the boards of the floor a spacious vault was discovered. It was high enough, for a man might sit upright in it with ease, and was separated from the cellar by a door and a narrow staircase. In this vault they found an electrical machine, a clock, and a little silver bell, which, as well as the electrical machine, was in communication with the altar and the crucifix that was fastened upon it. A hole had been made in the window-shutter opposite the chimney, which opened and shut with a slide. In this hole, as we learnt afterwards, was fixed a magic lantern, from which the figure of the ghost had been reflected on the opposite wall, over the chimney. From the garret and the cellar they brought several drums, to which large leaden bullets were fastened by strings; these had probably been used to imitate the roaring of thunder which we had heard.

On searching the Sicilian's clothes they found, in a case, different powders, genuine mercury in vials and boxes, phosphorus in a glass bottle, and a ring, which we immediately knew to be magnetic, because it adhered to a steel button that by accident had been placed near it. In his coat-pockets were found a rosary, a Jew's beard, a dagger, and a brace of pocket-pistols. "Let us see whether they are loaded," said one of the watch, and fired up the chimney.

"Jesus Maria!" cried a hollow voice, which we knew to be that of the first apparition, and at the same instant a bleeding person came tumbling down the chimney. "What! not yet laid, poor ghost!" cried the Englishman, while we started back in affright. "Home to thy grave. Thou hast appeared what thou wert not; now thou wilt become what thou didst but seem."

"Jesus Maria! I am wounded," repeated the man in the chimney. The ball had fractured his right leg. Care was immediately taken to have the wound dressed.

"But who art thou?" said the English lord; "and what evil spirit brought thee here?"

"I am a poor mendicant friar," answered the wounded man; "a strange gentleman gave me a zechin to--"

"Repeat a speech. And why didst thou not withdraw as soon as thy task was finished?"

I was waiting for a signal which we had agreed on to continue my speech; but as this signal was not given, I was endeavoring to get away, when I found the ladder had been removed.

"And what was the formula he taught thee?"

The wounded man fainted away; nothing more could be got from him. In the meantime the prince turned towards the principal officer of the watch, giving him at the same time some pieces of gold. "You have rescued us," said he, "from the hands of an impostor, and done us justice without even knowing who we were; would you increase our gratitude by telling us the name of the stranger who, by speaking only a few words, was able to procure us our liberty."

"Whom do you mean?" inquired the party addressed, with an air which plainly showed that the question was useless.

"The gentleman in a Russian uniform, who took you aside, showed you a written paper, and whispered a few words, in consequence of which you immediately set us free."

"Do not you know the gentleman? Was he not one of your company?"

"No," answered the prince; "and I have very important reasons for wishing to be more intimately acquainted with him."

"I know very little of him myself. Even his name is unknown to me, and I saw him to-day for the first time in my life."

"How? And was he in so short a time, and by using only a few words, able to convince you both of our innonocence and his own?"

"Undoubtedly, with a single word."

"And this was? I confess I wish to know it."

"This stranger, my prince," said the officer, weighing the zechins in his hand,--"you have been too generous for me to make a secret of it any longer,--this stranger is an officer of the Inquisition."

"Of the Inquisition? This man?"

"He is, indeed, gracious prince. I was convinced of it by the paper which he showed to me."

"This man, did you say? That cannot be."

"I will tell your highness more. It was upon his information that I have been sent here to arrest the sorcerer."

We looked at each other in the utmost astonishment.

"Now we know," said the English lord at length, "why the poor devil of a sorcerer started in such a terror when he looked more closely into his face. He knew him to be a spy, and that is why he uttered that shriek, and fell down before him."

"No!" interrupted the prince. "This man is whatever he wishes to be, and whatever the moment requires him to be. No mortal ever knew what he really was. Did you not see the knees of the Sicilian sink under him, when he said, with that terrible voice: 'Thou shalt summon no more ghosts?' There is something inexplicable in this matter. No person can persuade me that one man should be thus alarmed at the sight of another."

"The sorcerer himself will probably explain it the best," said the English lord, "if that gentleman," pointing to the officer, "will afford us an opportunity of speaking with his prisoner."

The officer consented to it, and, having agreed with the Englishman to visit the Sicilian in the morning, we returned to Venice.

[The Count O-------, whose narrative I have thus far literally copied, describes minutely the various effects of this adventure upon the mind of the prince and of his companions, and recounts a variety of tales of apparitions which this event gave occasion to introduce. I shall omit giving them to the reader, on the supposition that he is as curious as myself to know the conclusion of the adventure, and its effect on the conduct of the prince. I shall only add that the prince got no sleep the remainder of the night, and that he waited with impatience for the moment which was to disclose this incomprehensible mystery, Note of the German Editor.]

Lord Seymour (this was the name of the Englishman) called upon us very early in the forenoon, and was soon after followed by a confidential person whom the officer had entrusted with the care of conducting us to the prison.

I forgot to mention that one of the prince's domestics, a native of Bremen, who had served him many years with the strictest fidelity, and had entirely gained his confidence, had been missing for several days. Whether he had met with any accident, whether he had been kidnapped, or had voluntarily absented himself, was a secret to every one. The last supposition was extremely improbable, as his conduct had always been quiet and regular, and nobody had ever found fault with him. All that his companions could recollect was that he had been for some time very melancholy, and that, whenever he had a moment's leisure, he used to visit a certain monastery in the Giudecca, where he had formed an acquaintance with some monks.

This induced us to suppose that he might have fallen into the hands of the priests and had been persuaded to turn Catholic; and as the prince was very tolerant, or rather indifferent about matters of this kind, and the few inquiries he caused to be made proved unsuccessful, he gave up the search. He, however, regretted the loss of this man, who had constantly attended him in his campaigns, had always been faithfully attached to him, and whom it was therefore difficult to replace in a foreign country. The very same day the prince's banker, whom he had commissioned to provide him with another servant, was announced at the moment we were going out. He presented to the prince a middle-aged man, well-dressed, and of good appearance, who had been for a long time secretary to a procurator, spoke French and a little German, and was besides furnished with the best recommendations. The prince was pleased with the man's physiognomy; and as he declared that he would be satisfied with such wages as his service should be found to merit, the prince engaged him immediately.

We found the Sicilian in a private prison where, as the officer assured us, he had been lodged for the present, to accommodate the prince, before being removed to the lead roofs, to which there is no access. These lead roofs are the most terrible prisons in Venice. They are situated on the top of the palace of St. Mark, and the miserable criminals suffer so dreadfully from the heat of the leads occasioned by the heat of the burning rays of the sun descending directly upon them that they frequently become delirious.

The Sicilian had recovered from his yesterday's terror, and rose respectfully on seeing the prince enter. He had fetters on one hand and on one leg, but was able to walk about the room at liberty. The sentinel at the door withdrew as soon as we had entered.

"I come," said the prince, "to request an explanation of you on two subjects. You owe me the one, and it shall not be to your disadvantage if you grant me the other."

"My part is now acted," replied the Sicilian, "my destiny is in your hands." "Your sincerity alone can mitigate your punishment.

"Speak, honored prince, I am ready to answer you. I have nothing now to lose."

"You showed me the face of the Armenian in a looking-glass. How was this effected?"

"What you saw was no looking-glass. A portrait in crayons behind a glass, representing a man in an Armenian dress, deceived you. My quickness, the twilight, and your astonishment favored the deception. The picture itself must have been found among the other things seized at the inn."

"But how could you read my thoughts so accurately as to hit upon the Armenian?"

"This was not difficult, your highness. You must frequently have mentioned your adventure with the Armenian at table in the presence of your domestics. One of my accomplices accidentally got acquainted with one of your domestics in the Giudecca, and learned from him gradually as much as I wished to know."

"Where is the man?" asked the prince; "I have missed him, and doubtless you know of his desertion."

"I swear to your honor, sir, that I know not a syllable about it. I have never seen him myself, nor had any other concern with him than the one before mentioned."

"Proceed with your story," said the prince.

"By this means, also, I received the first information of your residence and of your adventures at Venice; and I resolved immediately to profit by them. You see, prince, I am sincere. I was apprised of your intended excursion on the Brenta. I prepared for it, and a key that dropped by chance from your pocket afforded me the first opportunity of trying my art upon you."

"How! Have I been mistaken? The adventure of the key was then a trick of yours, and not of the Armenian? You say this key fell from my pocket?"

"You accidentally dropped it in taking out your purse, and I seized an opportunity, when no one noticed me, to cover it with my foot. The person of whom you bought the lottery-ticket acted in concert with me. He caused you to draw it from a box where there was no blank, and the key had been in the snuff-box long before it came into your possession."

"I understand you. And the monk who stopped me in my way and addressed me in a manner so solemn."

"Was the same who, as I hear, has been wounded in the chimney. He is one of my accomplices, and under that disguise has rendered me many important services."

"But what purpose was this intended to answer?"

"To render you thoughtful; to inspire you with such a train of ideas as should be favorable to the wonders I intended afterwards to show you."

"The pantomimical dance, which ended in a manner so extraordinary, was at least none of your contrivance?"

"I had taught the girl who represented the queen. Her performance was the result of my instructions. I supposed your highness would be not a little astonished to find yourself known in this place, and (I entreat your pardon, prince) your adventure with the Armenian gave me reason to hope that you were already disposed to reject natural interpretations, and to attribute so marvellous an occurrence to supernatural agency."

"Indeed," exclaimed the prince, at once angry and amazed, and casting upon me a significant look; "indeed, I did not expect this."

[Neither did probably the greater number of my readers. The circumstance of the crown deposited at the feet of the prince, in a manner so solemn and unexpected, and the former prediction of the Armenian, seem so naturally and obviously to aim at the same object that at the first reading of these memoirs I immediately remembered the deceitful speech of the witches in Macbeth:--

"Hail to thee, Thane of Glamis! All hail, Macbeth! that shall be king hereafter!" and probably the same thing has occurred to many of my readers.

When a certain conviction has taken hold upon a man's mind in a solemn and extraordinary manner, it is sure to follow that all subsequent ideas which are in any way capable of being associated with this conviction should attach themselves to, and in some degree seem to be consequent upon it. The Sicilian, who seems to have had no other motive for his whole scheme than to astonish the prince by showing him that his rank was discovered, played, without being himself aware of it, the very game which most furthered the view of the Armenian; but however much of its interest this adventure will lose if I take away the higher motive which at first seemed to influence these actions, I must by no means infringe upon historical truth, but must relate the facts exactly as they occurred.--Note of the German Editor.]

"But," continued he, after a long silence, "how did you produce the figure which appeared on the wall over the chimney?"

"By means of a magic lantern that was fixed in the opposite window-shutter, in which you have undoubtedly observed an opening."

"But how did it happen that not one of us perceived the lantern?" asked Lord Seymour.

"You remember, my lord, that on your re-entering the room it was darkened by a thick smoke of frankincense. I likewise took the precaution to place the boards which had been taken up from the floor upright against the wall near the window. By these means I prevented the shutter from immediately attracting observation. Moreover, the lantern remained covered by a slide until you had taken your places, and there was no further reason to apprehend that you would institute any examination of the saloon."

"As I looked out of the window in the other pavilion," said I, "I fancied I heard a noise like that of a person placing a ladder against the side of the house. Was I right?"

"Exactly; it was the ladder upon which my assistants stood to direct the magic-lantern."

"The apparition," continued the prince, "had really a superficial likeness to my deceased friend, and what was particularly striking, his hair, which was of a very light color, was exactly imitated. Was this mere chance, or how did you come by such a resemblance?"

"Your highness must recollect that you had at table a snuff-box by your plate, with an enamelled portrait of an officer in a uniform. I asked whether you had anything about you as a memento of your friend, and as your highness answered in the affirmative, I conjectured that it might be the box. I had attentively examined the picture during supper, and being very expert in drawing and not less happy in taking likenesses, I had no difficulty in giving to my shade the superficial resemblance you have perceived, the more so as the marquis' features are very marked."

"But the figure seemed to move?"

"It appeared so, yet it was not the figure that moved but the smoke on which the light was reflected."

"And the man who fell down in the chimney spoke for the apparition?" "He did."

"But he could not hear your question distinctly."

"There was no occasion for it. Your highness will recollect that I cautioned you all very strictly not to propose any question to the apparition yourselves. My inquiries and his answers were preconcerted between us; and that no mistake might happen, I caused him to speak at long intervals, which he counted by the beating of a watch."

"You ordered the innkeeper carefully to extinguish every fire in the house with water; this was undoubtedly--"

"To save the man in the chimney from the danger of being suffocated; because the chimneys in the house communicate with each other, and I did not think myself very secure from your retinue."

"How did it happen," asked Lord Seymour, "that your ghost appeared neither sooner nor later than you wished him?"

"The ghost was in the room for some time before I called him, but while the room was lighted, the shade was too faint to be perceived. When the formula of the conjuration was finished, I caused the cover of the box, in which the spirit was burning, to drop down, the saloon was darkened, and it was not till then that the figure on the wall could be distinctly seen, although it had been reflected there a considerable time before."

"When the ghost appeared, we all felt an electric shock. How was that managed?"

"You have discovered the machine under the altar. You have also seen that I was standing upon a silk carpet. I directed you to form a half-moon around me, and to take each other's hands. When the crisis approached, I gave a sign to one of you to seize me by the hair. The silver crucifix was the conductor, and you felt the electric shock when I touched it with my hand."

"You ordered Count O----- and myself," continued Lord Seymour, "to hold two naked swords crossways over your head, during the whole time of the conjuration; for what purpose?"

"For no other than to engage your attention during the operation; because I distrusted you two the most. You remember, that I expressly commanded you to hold the sword one inch above my head; by confining you exactly to this distance, I prevented you from looking where I did not wish you. I had not then perceived my principal enemy."

"I own," cried Lord Seymour, "you acted with due precaution--but why were we obliged to appear undressed?"

"Merely to give a greater solemnity to the scene, and to excite your imaginations by the strangeness of the proceeding."

"The second apparition prevented your ghost from speaking," said the prince. "What should we have learnt from him?"

"Nearly the same as what you heard afterwards. It was not without design that I asked your highness whether you had told me everything that the deceased communicated to you, and whether you had made any further inquiries on this subject in his country. I thought this was necessary, in order to prevent the deposition of the ghost from being contradicted by facts with which you were previously acquainted. Knowing likewise that every man in his youth is liable to error, I inquired whether the life of your friend had been irreproachable, and on your answer I founded that of the ghost."

"Your explanation of this matter is satisfactory," resumed the prince, after a short silence; "but there remains a principal circumstance which I must ask you to clear up."

"If it be in my power, and--" "No conditions! Justice, in whose hands you now are, might perhaps not interrogate you with so much delicacy. Who was this unknown at whose feet we saw you fall? What do you know of him? How did you get acquainted with him? And in what way was he connected with the appearance of the second apparition?

"Your highness"--

"On looking at him more attentively, you gave a loud scream, and fell at his feet. What are we to understand by that?"

"This man, your highness"--He stopped, grew visibly perplexed, and with an embarrassed countenance looked around him. "Yes, prince, by all that is sacred, this unknown is a terrible being."

"What do you know of him? What connection have you with him? Do not hope to conceal the truth from us."

"I shall take care not to do so,--for who will warrant that he is not among us at this very moment?"

"Where? Who?" exclaimed we altogether, half-amused, half-startled, looking about the room. "That is impossible."

"Oh! to this man, or whatever he may be, things still more incomprehensible are possible."

"But who is he? Whence comes he? Is he an Armenian or a Russian? Of the characters be assumes, which is his real one?"

"He is nothing of what he appears to be. There are few conditions or countries of which he has not worn the mask. No person knows who he is, whence he comes, or whither he goes. That he has been for a long time in Egypt, as many pretend, and that he has brought from thence, out of a catacomb, his, occult sciences, I will neither affirm nor deny. Here we only know him by the name of the Incomprehensible. How old, for instance, do you suppose he is?"

"To judge from his appearance he can scarcely have passed forty." "And of what age do you suppose I am?"

"Not far from fifty."

"Quite right; and I must tell you that I was but a boy of seventeen when my grandfather spoke to me of this marvellous man whom he had seen at Famagusta; at which time he appeared nearly of the same age as he does at present."

"This is exaggerated, ridiculous, and incredible."

"By no means. Were I not prevented by these fetters I could produce vouchers whose dignity and respectability should leave you no room for doubt. There are several credible persons who remember having seen him, each, at the same time, in different parts of the globe. No sword can wound, no poison can hurt, no fire can burn him; no vessel in which he embarks can be wrecked. Time itself seems to lose its power over him. Years do not affect his constitution, nor age whiten his hair. Never was he seen to take any food. Never did he approach a woman. No sleep closes his eyes. Of the twenty-four hours in the day there is only one which he cannot command; during which no person ever saw him, and during which he never was employed in any terrestrial occupation."

"And this hour is?"

"The twelfth in the night. When the clock strikes twelve at midnight he ceases to belong to the living. In whatever place he is he must immediately be gone; whatever business he is engaged in he must instantly leave it. The terrible sound of the hour of midnight tears him from the arms of friendship, wrests him from the altar, and would drag him away even in the agonies of death. Whither he then goes, or what he is then engaged in, is a secret to every one. No person ventures to interrogate, still less to follow him. His features, at this dreadful hour, assume a sternness of expression so gloomy and terrifying that no person has courage sufficient to look him in the face, or to speak a word to him. However lively the conversation may have been, a dead silence immediately succeeds it, and all around wait for his return in respectful silence without venturing to quit their seats, or to open the door through which he has passed."

"Does nothing extraordinary appear in his person when he returns?" inquired one of our party.

"Nothing, except that he seems pale and exhausted, like a man who has just suffered a painful operation, or received some disastrous intelligence. Some pretend to have seen drops of blood on his linen, but with what degree of veracity I cannot affirm."

"Did no person ever attempt to conceal the approach of this hour from him, or endeavor to preoccupy his mind in such a manner as to make him forget it?"

"Once only, it is said, he missed the appointed time. The company was numerous and remained together late in the night. All the clocks and watches were purposely set wrong, and the warmth of conversation carried him away. When the stated hour arrived he suddenly became silent and motionless; his limbs continued in the position in which this instant had arrested them; his eyes were fixed; his pulse ceased to beat. All the means employed to awake him proved fruitless, and this situation endured till the hour had elapsed. He then revived on a sudden without any assistance, opened his eyes, and resumed his speech at the very syllable which he was pronouncing at the moment of interruption. The general consternation discovered to him what had happened, and he declared, with an awful solemnity, that they ought to think themselves happy in having escaped with the fright alone. The same night he quitted forever the city where this circumstance had occurred. The common opinion is that during this mysterious hour he converses with his genius. Some even suppose him to be one of the departed who is allowed to pass twenty-three hours of the day among the living, and that in the twenty-fourth his soul is obliged to return to the infernal regions to suffer its punishment. Some believe him to be the famous Apollonius of Tyana; and others the disciple of John, of whom it is said, 'He shall remain until the last judgment.'"

"A character so wonderful," replied the prince, "cannot fail to give rise to whimsical conjectures. But all this you profess to know only by hearsay, and yet his behavior to you and yours to him, seemed to indicate a more intimate acquaintance. Is it not founded upon some particular event in which you have yourself been concerned? Conceal nothing from us."

The Sicilian looked at us doubtingly and remained silent.

"If it concerns something," continued the prince, "that you do not wish to be made known, I promise you, in the name of these two gentlemen, the most inviolable secrecy. But speak candidly and without reserve."

"Could I hope," answered the prisoner, after a long silence, "that you would not make use of what I am going to relate as evidence against me, I would tell you a remarkable adventure of this Armenian, of which I myself was witness, and which will leave you no doubt of his supernatural powers. But I beg leave to conceal some of the names."

"Cannot you do it without this condition?"

"No, your highness. There is a family concerned in it whom I have reason to respect."

"Let us hear your story."

"It is about five years ago," began the Sicilian, "that at Naples, where I was practising my art with tolerable success, I became acquainted with a person of the name of Lorenzo del M-------, chevalier of the Order of St. Stephen, a young and rich nobleman, of one of the first families in the kingdom, who loaded me with kindnesses, and seemed to have a great esteem for my occult knowledge. He told me that the Marquis del M--nte, his father, was a zealous admirer of the cabala, and would think himself happy in having a philosopher like myself (for such he was pleased to call me) under his roof. The marquis lived in one of his country seats on the sea-shore, about seven miles from Naples. There, almost entirely secluded from the world, he bewailed, the loss of a beloved son, of whom he had been deprived by a terrible calamity. The chevalier gave me to understand that he and his family might perhaps have occasion to employ me on a matter of the most grave importance, in the hope of gaining through my secret science some information, to procure which all natural means had been tried in vain. He added, with a very significant look, that he himself might, perhaps at some future period, have reason to look upon me as the restorer of his tranquillity, and of all his earthly happiness. The affair was as follows:--

"This Lorenzo was the younger son of the marquis, and for that reason had been destined for the church; the family estates were to descend to the eldest. Jeronymo, which was the name of the latter, had spent many years on his travels, and had returned to his country about seven years prior to the event which I am about to relate, in order to celebrate his marriage with the only daughter of the neighboring Count C----tti. This marriage had been determined on by the parents during the infancy of the children, in order to unite the large fortunes of the two houses. But though this agreement was made by the two families, without consulting the hearts of the parties concerned, the latter had mutually pledged their faith to each other in secret. Jeronymo del M------ and Antonia C----- had been brought up together, and the little restraint imposed on two children, whom their parents were already accustomed to regard as destined for each other, soon produced between them a connection of the tenderest kind; the congeniality of their tempers cemented this intimacy; and in later years it ripened insensibly into love. An absence of four years, far from cooling this passion, had only served to inflame it; and Jeronymo returned to the arms of his intended bride as faithful and as ardent as if they had never been separated.

"The raptures occasioned by his return had not yet subsided, and the preparations for the happy day were advancing with the utmost zeal and activity, when the bridegroom disappeared. He used frequently to pass whole afternoons in a summer-house which commanded a prospect of the sea, and was accustomed to take the diversion of sailing on the water. One day, on an evening spent in this manner, it was observed that he remained absent a much longer time than usual, and his friends began to be very uneasy on his account. Messengers were despatched after him, vessels were sent to sea in quest of him; no person had seen him. None of his servants were missed; he must, therefore, have gone alone. Night came on, and he did not appear. The next morning dawned; the day passed, the evening succeeded--, Jeronymo came not. Already they had begun to give themselves up to the most melancholy conjectures when the news arrived that an Algerine pirate had landed the preceeding day on that coast, and carried off several of the inhabitants. Two galleys which were ready for sea were immediately manned; the old marquis himself embarked in one of them, to attempt the deliverance of his son at the peril of his own life. On the third morning they perceived the corsair. They had the advantage of the wind; they were just about to overtake the pirate, and had even approached so near that Lorenzo, who was in one of the galleys, fancied that he saw upon the deck of the adversary's ship a signal made by his brother, when a sudden storm separated the vessels. Hardly could the damaged galleys sustain the fury of the tempest. The pirate in the meantime had disappeared, and the distressed state of the other vessels obliged them to land at Malta.

The affliction of the family knew no bounds. The distracted old marquis tore his gray hairs in the utmost violence of grief; and fears were entertained for the life of the young countess. Five years were consumed in fruitless inquiries. Diligent search was made along all the coast of Barbary; immense sums were offered for the ransom of the poor marquis, but no person came forward to claim them. The only probable conjecture which remained for the family to form was, that the same storm which had separated the galleys from the pirate had destroyed the latter, and that the whole ship's company had perished in the waves.

"But, however this supposition might be, it did not by any means amount to a certainty, and could not authorize the family altogether to renounce the hope that the lost Jeronymo might again appear. In case, however, that he was really dead, either the family must become extinct, or the younger son must relinquish the church, and assume the rights of the elder. As justice, on the one hand, seemed to oppose the latter measure, so, on the other hand, the necessity of preserving the family from annihilation required that the scruple should not be carried too far. In the meantime through grief and the infirmities of age, the old marquis was fast sinking to his grave; every unsuccessful attempt diminished the hope of finding his lost son; he saw the danger of his family's becoming extinct, which might be obviated by a trifling injustice on his part, in consenting to favor his younger son at the expense of the elder. The consummation of his alliance with the house of Count C---tti required only that a name should be changed, for the object of the two families was equally accomplished, whether Antonia became the wife of Lorenzo or of Jeronymo. The faint probability of the latter's appearing again weighed but little against the certain and pressing danger of the total extinction of the family, and the old marquis, who felt the approach of death every day more and more, ardently wished at least to die free from this inquietude.

"Lorenzo, however, who was to be principally benefited by this measure, opposed it with the greatest obstinacy. Alike unmoved by the allurements of an immense fortune, and the attractions of the beautiful and accomplished being whom his family were about to deliver into his arms, he refused, on principles the most generous and conscientious, to invade the rights of a brother, who perhaps was still alive, and might some day return to claim his own. 'Is not the lot of my dear Jeronymo,' said he, 'made sufficiently miserable by the horrors of a long captivity, that I should yet add bitterness to his cup of grief by stealing from him all that he holds most dear? With what conscience could I supplicate heaven for his return when his wife is in my arms? With what countenance could I hasten to meet him should he at last be restored to us by some miracle? And even supposing that he is torn from us forever, how can we better honor his memory than by keeping constantly open the chasm which his death has caused in our circle? Can we better show our respect to him than by sacrificing our dearest hopes upon his tomb, and keeping untouched, as a sacred deposit, what was peculiarly his own?'

"But all the arguments which fraternal delicacy could adduce were insufficient to reconcile the old marquis to the idea of being obliged to witness the extinction of a pedigree which nine centuries had beheld flourishing. All that Lorenzo could obtain was a respite of two years before leading the affianced bride of his brother to the altar. During this period they continued their inquiries with the utmost diligence. Lorenzo himself made several voyages, and exposed his person to many dangers. No trouble, no expense was spared to recover the lost Jeronymo. These two years, however, like those which preceded them, were in vain?"

"And the Countess Antonia?" said the prince, "You tell us nothing of her. Could she so calmly submit to her fate? I cannot suppose it."

34

"Antonia," answered the Sicilian, "experienced the most violent struggle between duty and inclination, between hate and admiration. The disinterested generosity of a brother's love affected her; she felt herself forced to esteem a person whom she could never love. Her heart was torn by conflicting sentiments. But her repugnance to the chevalier seemed to increase in the same degree as his claims upon her esteem augmented.

Lorenzo perceived with heartfelt sorrow the grief that consumed her youth. A tender compassion insensibly assumed the place of that indifference with which, till then, he had been accustomed to regard her; but this treacherous sentiment quickly deceived him, and an ungovernable passion began by degrees to shake the steadiness of his virtue--a virtue which, till then, had been unequalled.

"He, however, still obeyed the dictates of generosity, though at the expense of his love. By his efforts alone was the unfortunate victim protected against the arbitrary proceedings of the rest of the family. But his endeavors were ineffectual. Every victory he gained over his passion rendered him more worthy of Antonia; and the disinterestedness with which he refused her left her no excuse for resistance.

"This was the state of affairs when the chevalier engaged me to visit him at his father's villa. The earnest recommendation of my patron procured me a reception which exceeded my most sanguine hopes. I must not forget to mention that by some remarkable operations I had previously rendered my name famous in different lodges of Freemasons, which circumstance may, perhaps, have contributed to strengthen the old marquis' confidence in me, and to heighten his expectations. I beg you will excuse me from describing particularly the lengths I went with him, and the means which I employed; you may judge of them from what I have already confessed to you.

Profiting by the mystic books which I found in his very extensive library, I was soon able to converse with him in his own language, and to adorn my system of the invisible world with the most extraordinary inventions. In a short time I could make him believe whatever I pleased, and he would have sworn as readily as upon an article in the canon. Moreover, as he was very devout, and was by nature somewhat credulous, my fables received credence the more readily, and in a short time I had so completely surrounded and hemmed him in with mystery that he cared for nothing that was not supernatural. In short I became the patron saint of the house. The usual subject of my lectures was the exaltation of human nature, and the intercourse of men with superior beings; the infallible Count Gabalis was my oracle.

[A mystical work of that title, written in French in 1670 by the Abbe do Villars, and translated into English in 1600. Pope is said to have borrowed from it the machinery of his Rape of the Lock.-H. G. B.]

"The young countess, whose mind since the loss of her lover had been more occupied in the world of spirits than in that of nature, and who had, moreover, a strong shade of melancholy in her composition, caught my hints with a fearful satisfaction. Even the servants contrived to have some business in the room when I was speaking, and seizing now and then one of my expressions, joined the fragments together in their own way.

"Two months were passed in this manner at the marquis' villa, when the chevalier one morning entered my apartment. A deep sorrow was painted on his countenance, his features were convulsed, he threw himself into a chair, with gestures of despair.

"'Captain,' said he, 'it is all over with me, I must begone; I can remain here no longer.'

"'What is the matter, chevalier? What ails you?'

"'Oh! this fatal passion!' said he, starting frantically from his chair. 'I have combated it like a man; I can resist it no longer.'

"'And whose fault is it but yours, my dear chevalier? Are they not all in your favor? Your father, your relations.'

"'My father, my relations! What are they to me? I want not a forced union, but one of inclination, Have not I a rival? Alas! and what a rival! Perhaps among the dead! Oh! let me go! Let me go to the end of the world,--I must find my brother.'

"'What! after so many unsuccessful attempts can you still cherish hope?'

"'Hope!' replied the chevalier; 'alas! no. It has long since vanished from my heart, but it has not from hers. Of what consequence are my sentiments?

Can I be happy while there remains a gleam of hope in Antonia's heart? Two words, my friend, would end my torments. But it is in vain. My destiny must continue to be miserable till eternity shall break its long silence, and the grave shall speak in my behalf.'

"'Is it then a state of certainty that would render you happy?'

"'Happy! Alas! I doubt whether I can ever again be happy. But uncertainty is of all others the most dreadful pain.'

"After a short interval of silence he suppressed his emotion, and continued mournfully, 'If he could but see my torments! Surely a constancy which renders his brother miserable cannot add to his happiness. Can it be just that the living should suffer so much for the sake of the dead, who can no longer enjoy earthly felicity? If he knew the pangs I suffer,' continued he, hiding his face on my shoulder, while the tears streamed from his eyes, 'yes, perhaps he himself would conduct her to my arms.'

"'But is there no possibility of gratifying your wishes?' "He started. 'What do you say, my friend?'

"'Less important occasions than the present,' said I, 'have disturbed the repose of the dead for the sake of the living. Is not the whole earthly happiness of a man, of a brother--'

"'The whole earthly happiness! Ah, my friend, I feel what you say is but too true; my entire felicity.'

"'And the tranquillity of a distressed family, are not these sufficient to justify such a measure? Undoubtedly. If any sublunary concern can authorize us to interrupt the peace of the blessed, to make use of a power--'

"'For God's sake, my friend,' said he, interrupting me, no more of this. Once, I avow it, I had such a thought; I think I mentioned it to you; but I have long since rejected it as horrid and abominable.'

"You will have conjectured already," continued the Sicilian, "to what this conversation led us. I endeavored to overcome the scruples of the chevalier, and at last succeeded. We resolved to summon the spirit of the deceased Jeronymo. I only stipulated for the delay of a fortnight, in order, as I pretended, to prepare myself in a suitable manner for so solemn an act. The time being expired, and my machinery in readiness, I took advantage of a very gloomy day, when we were all assembled as usual, to obtain the consent of the family, or rather, gradually to lead them to the subject, so that they themselves requested it of me. The most difficult part of the task was to obtain the approbation of Antonia, whose presence was most essential. My endeavors were, however, greatly assisted by the melancholy turn of her mind, and perhaps still more so by a faint hope that Jeronymo might still be living, and therefore would not appear. A want of confidence in the thing itself, or a doubt of my ability, was the only obstacle which I had not to contend with.

"Having obtained the consent of the family, the third day was fixed on for the operation. I prepared them for the solemn transaction by mystical instruction, by fasting, solitude, and prayers, which I ordered to be continued till late in the night. Much use was also made of a certain musical instrument, unknown till that time, and which, in such cases, has often been found very powerful. The effect of these artifices was so much beyond my expectation that the enthusiasm to which on this occasion I was obliged to force myself was infinitely heightened by that of my audience. The anxiously-expected hour at last arrived."

"I guess," said the prince, "whom you are now going to introduce. But go on, go on."

"No, your highness. The incantation succeeded according to my wishes." "How? Where is the Armenian?"

"Do not fear, your highness. He will appear but too soon. I omit the description of the farce itself, as it would lead me to too great a length. Be it sufficient to say that it answered my utmost expectations. The old marquis, the young countess, her mother, Lorenzo, and a few others of the family, were present. You may imagine that during my long residence in this house I had not wanted opportunities of gathering information respecting everything that concerned the deceased. Several portraits of him enabled me to give the apparition the most striking likeness, and as I suffered the ghost to speak only by signs, the sound of his voice could excite no suspicion.

"The departed Jeronymo appeared--in the dress of a Moorish slave, with a deep wound in his neck. You observe that in this respect I was counteracting the general supposition that he had perished in the waves, for I had reason to hope that the unexpectedness of this circumstance would heighten their belief in the apparition itself, while, on the other hand, nothing appeared to me more dangerous than to keep too strictly to what was natural."

"I think you judged rightly," said the prince. "In whatever respects apparitions the most probable is the least acceptable. If their communications are easily comprehended we undervalue the channel by which they are obtained. Nay, we even suspect the reality of the miracle if the discoveries which it brings to light are such as might easily have been imagined. Why should we disturb the repose of a spirit if it is to inform us of nothing more than the ordinary powers of the intellect are capable of teaching us? But, on the other hand, if the intelligence which we receive is extraordinary and unexpected it confirms in some degree the miracle by which it is obtained; for who can doubt an operation to be supernatural when its effect could not be produced by natural means? I interrupt you," added the prince. "Proceed in your narrative."

"I asked the ghost whether there was anything in this world which he still considered as his own," continued the Sicilian, "and whether he had left anything behind that was particularly dear to him? The ghost shook his head three times, and lifted up his hand towards heaven. Previous to his retiring he dropped a ring from his finger, which was found on the floor after he had disappeared. Antonia took it, and, looking at it attentively, she knew it to be the ring she had given her intended husband on their betrothal."

"The ring!" exclaimed the prince, surprised. "How did you get it?"

"Who? I? It was not the true one, your highness; I got it. It was only a counterfeit."

"A counterfeit!" repeated the prince. "But in order to counterfeit you required the true one. How did you come by it? Surely the deceased never went without it."

"That is true," replied the Sicilian, with symptoms of confusion. "But from a description which was given me of the genuine ring--"

"A description which was given you! By whom?"

"Long before that time. It was a plain gold ring, and had, I believe, the name of the young countess engraved on it. But you made me lose the connection."

"What happened further?" said the prince, with a very dissatisfied countenance.

"The family felt convinced that Jeronymo was no more. From that day forward they publicly announced his death, and went into mourning. The circumstance of the ring left no doubt, even in the mind of Antonia, and added a considerable weight to the addresses of the chevalier.

"In the meantime the violent shock which the young countess had received from the sight of the apparition brought on her a disorder so dangerous that the hopes of Lorenzo were very near being destroyed forever. On her recovery she insisted upon taking the veil; and it was only at the most serious remonstrances of her confessor, in whom she placed implicit confidence, that she was induced to abandon her project. At length the united solicitations of the family, and of the confessor, forced from her a reluctant consent. The last day of mourning was fixed on for the day of marriage, and the old marquis determined to add to the solemnity of the occasion by making over all his estates to his lawful heir.

"The day arrived, and Lorenzo received his trembling bride at the altar. In the evening a splendid banquet was prepared for the cheerful guests in a hall superbly illuminated, and the most lively and delightful music contributed to increase the general gladness. The happy old marquis wished all the world to participate in his joy. All the entrances of the palace were thrown open, and every one who sympathized in his happiness was joyfully welcomed. In the midst of the throng--"

The Sicilian paused. A trembling expectation suspended our breath.

"In-the midst of the throng," continued the prisoner, "appeared a Franciscan monk, to whom my attention was directed by the person who sat next to me at table. He was standing motionless like a marble pillar. His shape was tall and thin; his face pale and ghastly; his eyes were fixed with a grave and mournful expression on the new-married couple. The joy which beamed on the face of every one present appeared not on his. His countenance never once varied. He seemed like a statue among the living. Such an object, appearing amidst the general joy, struck me more forcibly from its contrast with everything around. It left on my mind so indelible an impression that from it alone I have been enabled (which would otherwise have been impossible) to recollect the features of the Franciscan monk in the Russian officer; for, without doubt, you must have already conceived that the person I have described was no other than your Armenian.

40

"I frequently attempted to withdraw my eyes from this terrible figure, but they wandered back involuntarily, and found his countenance unaltered. I pointed him out to the person who sat nearest to me on the other side, and he did the same to the person next to him. In a few minutes a general curiosity and astonishment pervaded the whole company. The conversation languished; a general silence succeeded; the monk did not heed it. He continued motionless as before; his grave and mournful looks constantly fixed upon the new-married couple; his appearance struck every one with terror. The young countess alone, who found the transcript of her own sorrow in the fact of the stranger, beheld with a melancholy satisfaction the only object that seemed to understand and sympathize in her sufferings.

The crowd insensibly diminished. It was past midnight; the music became fainter and more languid; the tapers grew dim, and many of them went out. The conversation, declining by degrees, lost itself at last in secret murmurs, and the faintly illuminated hall was nearly deserted. The monk, in the meantime, continued motionless, with the same grave and mournful look still fixed on the new-married couple. The company at length rose from the table; the guests dispersed; the family assembled in a separate group, and the monk, though uninvited, continued near them. How it happened that no person spoke to him I cannot conceive.

"The female friends now surrounded the trembling bride, who cast a supplicating and distressed look on the venerable stranger; he did not answer it. The gentlemen assembled in the same manner around the bridegroom. A solemn and anxious silence prevailed among them. 'That we should be so happy here together,' began at length the old marquis, who alone seemed not to behold the stranger, or at least seemed to behold him without dismay. 'That we should be so happy here together, and my son Jeronymo cannot be with us!'

"'Have you invited him, and has he failed to come?' asked the monk. It was the first time he had spoken. We looked at him in alarm.

"'Alas! he is gone to a place from whence there is no return,' answered the old man. 'Reverend father I you misunderstood me. My son Jeronymo is dead.'

"'Perhaps he only fears to appear in this company,' replied the monk. 'Who knows how your son Jeronymo may be situated? Let him now hear the voice which he heard the last. Desire your son Lorenzo to call him.'

"'What means he?' whispered the company to one another. Lorenzo changed color. I will not deny that my own hair began to stand on end.

"In the meantime the monk approached a sideboard; he took a glass of wine and carried to his lips. 'To the memory of our dear Jeronymo!' said he. 'Let every one who loved the deceased follow my example.'

"'Be you who you may, reverend father!' exclaimed the old marquis, 'you have pronounced a name dear to us all, and you are heartily welcome here;' then turning to us, he offered us full glasses. 'Come, my friends!' continued he, 'let us not be surpassed by a stranger. The memory of my son Jeronymo!'

"Never, I believe, was any toast less heartily received.

"'There is one glass still unemptied," said the marquis. 'Why does my son Lorenzo refuse to drink this friendly toast?'

"Lorenzo, trembling, received the glass from the hands of the monk; tremblingly he put it to his lips.'To my dearly-beloved brother Jeronymo!' he stammered out, and replaced the glass with a shudder.

"'That was my murderer's voice!' exclaimed a terrible figure, which appeared suddenly in the midst of us, covered with blood, and disfigured with horrible wounds.

"Do not ask me the rest," added the Sicilian, with every symptom of horror in his countenance. "I lost my senses the moment I looked at this apparition. The same happened to every one present. When we recovered the monk and the ghost had disappeared; Lorenzo was writhing in the agonies of death. He was carried to bed in the most dreadful convulsions.

No person attended him but his confessor and the sorrowful old marquis, in whose presence he expired. The marquis died a few weeks after him.

Lorenzo's secret is locked in the bosom of the priest who received his last confession; no person ever learnt what it was.

"Soon after this event a well was cleaned in the farmyard of the marquis' villa. It had been disused for many years, and was almost closed up by shrubs and old trees. On digging among the rubbish a human skeleton was found. The house where this happened is now no more; the family del M-----nte is extinct, and Antonia's tomb may be seen in a convent not far from Salerno.

"You see," continued the Sicilian, seeing us all stand silent and thoughtful, "you see how my acquaintance with this Russian officer, Armenian, or Franciscan friar originated. Judge now whether I had not good cause to tremble at the sight of a being who has twice placed himself in my way in a manner so terrible."

"I beg you will answer me one question more," said the prince, rising from his seat. "Have you been always sincere in your account of everything relating to the chevalier?"

"To the best of my knowledge I have," replied the Sicilian. "You really believed him to be an honest man?"

"I did; by heaven! I did," answered he again. "Even at the tine he gave you the ring?"

"How! He gave me no ring. I did not say that he gave me the ring."

"Very well!" said the prince, pulling the bell, and preparing to depart. "And you believe" (going back to the prisoner) "that the ghost of the Marquis de Lanoy, which the Russian officer introduced after your apparition, was a true and real ghost?"

"I cannot think otherwise."

"Let us go!" said the prince, addressing himself to us. The gaoler came in. "We have done," said the prince to him. "You, sir," turning to the prisoner, "you shall hear further from me."

"I am tempted to ask your highness the last question you proposed to the sorcerer," said I to the prince, when we were alone. "Do you believe the second ghost to have been a real and true one?"

"I believe it! No, not now, most assuredly." "Not now? Then you did once believe it?"

"I confess I was tempted for a moment to believe it something more than the contrivance of a juggler."

"And I could wish to see the man who under similar circumstances would not have had the same impression. But what reasons have you for retracting your opinion? What the prisoner has related of the Armenian ought to increase rather than diminish your belief in his super natural powers."

"What this wretch has related of him," said the prince, interrupting me very gravely. "I hope," continued he, "you have now no doubt but that we have had to do with a villain."

"No; but must his evidence on that account--" "The evidence of a villain, even supposing I had no other reason for doubt, can have no weight against common sense and established truth. Does a man who has already deceived me several times, and whose trade it is to deceive, does he deserve to be heard in a cause in which the unsupported testimony of even the most sincere adherent to truth could not be received? Ought we to believe a man who perhaps never once spoke truth for its own sake? Does such a man deserve credit, when he appears as evidence against human reason and the eternal laws of nature? Would it not be as absurd as to admit the accusation of a person notoriously infamous against unblemished and irreproachable innocence?"

"But what motives could he have for giving so great a character to a man whom he has so many reasons to hate?"

"I am not to conclude that he can have no motives for doing this because I am unable to comprehend them. Do I know who has bribed him to deceive me? I confess I cannot penetrate the whole contexture of his plan; but he has certainly done a material injury to the cause he advocates by proving himself to be at least an impostor, and perhaps something worse."

"The circumstance of the ring, I allow, appears somewhat suspicions."

"It is more than suspicious," answered the prince; "it is decisive. He received this ring from the murderer, and at the moment he received it he must have been certain that it was from the murderer. Who but the assassin, could have taken from the finger of the deceased a ring which he undoubtedly never took off himself? Throughout the whole of his narration the Sicilian has labored to persuade us that while he was endeavoring to deceive Lorenzo, Lorenzo was in reality deceiving him. Would he have had recourse to this subterfuge if he had not been sensible how much he should lose in our estimation by confessing himself an accomplice with the assassin? The whole story is visibly nothing but a series of impostures, invented merely to connect the few truths he has thought proper to give us. Ought I then to hesitate in disbelieving the eleventh assertion of a person who has already deceived me ten times, rather than admit a violation of the fundamental laws of nature, which I have ever found in the most perfect harmony?"

"I have nothing to reply to all this, but the apparition we saw yesterday is to me not the less incomprehensible."

"It is also incomprehensible to me, although I have been tempted to believe that I have found a key to it."

"How so?" asked I.

"Do not you recollect that the second apparition, as soon as he entered, walked directly up to the altar, took the crucifix in his hand, and placed himself upon the carpet?"

"It appeared so to me."

"And this crucifix, according to the Sicilian's confession, was a conductor. You see that the apparition hastened to make himself electrical. Thus the blow which Lord Seymour struck him with a sword was of course ineffectual; the electric stroke disabled his arm."

"This is true with respect to the sword. But the pistol fired by the Sicilian, the ball of which we heard roll slowly upon the altar?"

"Are you convinced that this was the same ball which was fired from the pistol?" replied the prince. "Not to mention that the puppet, or the man who represented the ghost, may have been so well accoutred as to be invulnerable by sword or bullet; but consider who it was that loaded the pistols."

"True," said I, and a sudden light broke upon my mind; "the Russian officer had loaded them, but it was in our presence. How could he have deceived us?"

"Why should he not have deceived us? Did you suspect him sufficiently to observe him? Did you examine the ball before it was put into the pistol?

May it not have been one of quicksilver or clay? Did you take notice whether the Russian officer really put it into the barrel, or dropped it into his other hand? But supposing that he actually loaded the pistols, what is to convince you that he really took the loaded ones into the room where the ghost appeared, and did not change them for another pair, which he might have done the more easily as nobody ever thought of noticing him, and we were besides occupied in undressing? And could not the figure, at the moment when we were prevented from seeing it by the smoke of the pistol, have dropped another ball, with which it had been beforehand provided, on the the altar? Which of these conjectures is impossible?"

"You are right. But that striking resemblance to your deceased friend! I have often seen him with you, and I immediately recognized him in the apparition."

"I did the same, and I must confess the illusion was complete. But if the juggler from a few stolen glances at my snuff-box was able to give to his apparition a resemblance, what was to prevent the Russian officer, who had used the box during the whole time of supper, who had had liberty to observe the picture unnoticed, and to whom I had discovered in confidence whom it represented, what was to prevent him from doing the same? Add to this what has been before observed by the Sicilian, that the prominent features of the marquis were so striking as to be easily imitated; what is there so inexplicable in this second ghost?"

"But the words he uttered? The information he gave you about your friend?"

"What?" said the prince, "Did not the Sicilian assure us, that from the little which he had learnt from me he had composed a similar story? Does not this prove that the invention was obvious and natural? Besides, the answers of the ghost, like those of an oracle, were so obscure that he was in no danger of being detected in a falsehood. If the man who personated the ghost possessed sagacity and presence of mind, and knew ever-so-little of the affair on which he was consulted, to what length might not he have carried the deception?"

"Pray consider, your highness, how much preparation such a complicated artifice would have required from the Armenian; how much time it takes to paint a face with sufficient exactness; how much time would have been requisite to instruct the pretended ghost, so as to guard him against gross errors; what a degree of minute attention to regulate every minor attendant or adventitious circumstance, which must be answered in some manner, lest they should prove detrimental! And remember that the Russian officer was absent but half an hour. Was that short space of time sufficient to make even such arrangements as were most indispensable? Surely, my prince, not even a dramatic writer, who has the least desire to preserve the three terrible unities of

Aristotle, durst venture to load the interval between one act and another with such a variety of action, or to presume upon such a facility of belief in his audience."

"What! You think it absolutely impossible that every necessary preparation should have been made in the space of half an hour?"

"Indeed, I look upon it as almost impossible."

"I do not understand this expression. Does it militate against the physical laws of time and space, or of matter and motion, that a man so ingenious and so expert as this Armenian must undoubtedly be, assisted by agents whose dexterity and acuteness are probably not inferior to his own; favored by the time of night, and watched by no one, provided with such means and instruments as a man of this profession is never without --is it impossible that such a man, favored by such circumstances, should be able to effect so much in so short a time? Is it ridiculous or absurd to suppose, that by a very small number of words or signs he can convey to his assistants very extensive commissions, and direct very complex operations? Nothing ought to be admitted that is contrary to the established laws of nature, unless it is something with which these laws are absolutely incompatible. Would you rather give credit to a miracle than admit an improbability? Would you solve a difficulty rather by overturning the powers of nature than by believing an artful and uncommon combination of them?"

"Though the fact will not justify a conclusion such as you have condemned, you must, however, grant that it is far beyond our conception."

"I am almost tempted to dispute even this," said the prince, with a quiet smile. "What would you say, my dear count, if it should be proved, for instance, that the operations of the Armenian were prepared and carried on, not only during the half-hour that he was absent from us, not only in haste and incidentally, but during the whole evening and the whole night? You recollect that the Sicilian employed nearly three hours in preparation."

"The Sicilian? Yes, my prince."

"And how will you convince me that this juggler had not as much concern in the second apparition as in the first?"

"How so, your highness?"

"That he was not the principal assistant of the Armenian? In a word, how will you convince me that they did not co-operate?"

"It would be a difficult task to prove that," exclaimed I, with no little surprise.

"Not so difficult, my dear count, as you imagine. What! Could it have happened by mere chance that these two men should form a design so extraordinary and so complicated upon the same person, at the same time, and in the same place? Could mere chance have produced such an exact harmony between their operations, that one of them should play so exactly the game of the other? Suppose for a moment that the Armenian intended to heighten the effect of his deception, by introducing it after a less refined one--that he created a Hector to make himself his Achilles. Suppose that he has done all this to discover what degree of credulity he could expect to find in me, to examine the readiest way to gain my confidence, to familiarize himself with his subject by an attempt that might have miscarried without any prejudice to his plan; in a word, to tune the instrument on which he intended to play. Suppose he did this with the view of exciting my suspicions on one subject in order to divert my attention from another more important to his design. Lastly, suppose he wishes to have some indirect methods of information, which he had himself occasion to practise, imputed to the sorcerer, in order to divert suspicion from the true channel."

"How do you mean?" said I.

"Suppose, for instance, that he may have bribed some of my servants to give him secret intelligence, or, perhaps, even some papers which may serve his purpose. I have missed one of my domestics. What reason have I to think that the Armenian is not concerned in his leaving me? Such a connection, however, if it existed, may be accidently discovered; a letter may be intercepted; a servant, who is in the secret, may betray his trust.

Now all the consequence of the Armenian is destroyed if I detect the source of his omniscience. He therefore introduces this sorcerer, who must be supposed to have some design upon me. He takes care to give me early notice of him and his intentions, so that whatever I may hereafter discover my suspicions must necessarily rest upon the Sicilian. This is the puppet with which he amuses me, whilst he himself, unobserved and unsuspected, is entangling me in invisible snares."

"We will allow this. But is it consistent with the Armenian's plan that he himself should destroy the illusion which he has created, and disclose the mysteries of his science to the eyes of the uninitiated?"

"What mysteries does he disclose? None, surely, which he intends to practise on me. He therefore loses nothing by the discovery. But, on the other hand, what an advantage will he gain, if this pretended victory over juggling and deception should render me secure and unsuspecting; if he succeeds in diverting my attention from the right quarter, and in fixing my wavering suspicions on an object the most remote from the real one! He could naturally expect that, sooner or later, either from my own doubts, or at the suggestion of another, I should be tempted to seek a key to his mysterious wonders, in the mere art of a juggler; how could he better provide against such an inquiry than by contrasting his prodigies with juggling tricks. By confining the latter within artificial limits, and by delivering, as it were, into my hands a scale by which to appreciate them, he naturally exalts and perplexes my ideas of the former. How many suspicions he precludes by this single contrivance! How many methods of accounting for his miracles, which afterwards have occurred to me, does he refute beforehand!"

"But in exposing such a finished deception he has acted very much against his own interest, both by quickening the penetration of those whom he meant to impose upon, and by staggering their belief in miracles in general. Your highness' self is the best proof of the insufficiency of his plan, if indeed he ever had one."

"Perhaps he has been mistaken in respect to myself," said the prince; "but his conclusions have nevertheless been well founded. Could he foresee that I should exactly notice the very circumstance which threatens to become the key to the whole artifice? Was it in his plan that the creature he employed should render himself thus vulnerable? Are we certain that the Sicilian has not far exceeded his commission? He has undoubtedly done so with respect to the ring, and yet it is chiefly this single circumstance which determined my distrust in him. How easily may a plan, whose contexture is most artful and refined, be spoiled in the execution by an awkward instrument. It certainly was not the Armenian's intention that the sorcerer should trumpet his fame to us in the style of a mountebank, that he should endeavor to impose upon us such fables as are too gross to bear the least reflection. For instance, with what countenance could this impostor affirm that the miraculous being he spoke of must renounce all commerce with mankind at twelve in the night? Did we not see him among us at that very hour?"

"That is true," cried I. "He must have forgotten it."

"It often happens, to people of this description, that they overact their parts; and, by aiming at too much, mar the effects which a well-managed deception is calculated to produce."

"I cannot, however, yet prevail on myself to look upon the whole as a mere preconcerted scheme. What! the Sicilian's terror, his convulsive fits, his swoon, the deplorable situation in which we saw him, and which was even such as to move our pity, were all these nothing more than a studied part? I allow that a skilful performer may carry imitation to a very high pitch, but he certainly has no power over the organs of life."

"As for that, my friend," replied the prince, "I have seen Richard III. performed by Garrick. But were we at that moment sufficiently cool to be capable of observing dispassionately? Could we judge of the emotion of the Sicilian when we were almost overcome by our own? Besides, the decisive crisis even of a deception is so momentous to the deceiver himself that excessive anxiety may produce in him symptoms as violent as those which surprise excites in the deceived. Add to this the unexpected entrance of the watch."

"I am glad you remind me of that, prince. Would the Armenian have ventured to discover such a dangerous scheme to the eye of justice; to expose the fidelity of his creature to so severe a test? And for what purpose?"

"Leave that matter to him; he is no doubt acquainted with the people he employs. Do we know what secret crimes may have secured him the silence of this man? You have been informed of the office he holds in Venice; what difficulty will he find in saving a man of whom he himself is the only accuser?"

[This suggestion of the prince was but too well justified by the event. For, some days after, on inquiring after the prisoner, we were told that he had escaped, and had not since been heard of.]

"You ask what could be his motives for delivering this man into the hands of justice?" continued the prince. "By what other method, except this violent one, could he have wrested from the Sicilian such an infamous and improbable confession, which, however, was so material to the success of his plan? Who but a man whose case is desperate, and who has nothing to lose, would consent to give so humiliating an account of himself? Under what other circumstances could we have believed such a confession?"

"I grant all this, my prince. That the two apparitions were mere contrivances of art; that the Sicilian has imposed upon us a tale which the Armenian his master, had previously taught him; that the efforts of both have been directed to the same end, and, from this mutual intelligence all the wonderful incidents which have astonished us in this adventure may be easily explained. But the prophecy in the square of St. Mark, that first miracle, which, as it were, opened the door to all the rest, still remains unexplained; and of what use is the key to all his other wonders if we despair of resolving this single one?"

"Rather invert the proposition, my dear count," answered the prince, "and say what do all these wonders prove if I can demonstrate that a single one among them is a juggling trick? The prediction, I own, is totally beyond my conception. If it stood alone; if the Armenian had closed the scene with it, instead of beginning it, I confess I do not know how far I might have been carried. But in the base alloy with which it is mixed it is certainly rather suspicious. Time may explain, or not explain it; but believe me, my friend!" added the prince, taking my hand, with a grave countenance,--"a man who can command supernatural powers has no occasion to employ the arts of a juggler; he despises them."

"Thus," says Count O------, "ended a conversation which I have related word for word, because it shows the difficulties which were to be overcome before the prince could be effectually imposed upon; and I hope it may free his memory from the imputation of having blindly and inconsiderately thrown himself into a snare, which was spread for his destruction by the most unexampled and diabolical wickedness. Not all," continues Count

O------, "who, at the moment I am writing, smile contemptuously at the prince's credulity, and, in the fancied superiority of their own yet untempted understanding, unconditionally condemn him; not all of these, I apprehend, would have stood his first trial so courageously. If afterwards, notwithstanding this providential warning, we witness his downfall; if we see that the black design against which, at the very outset, he was thus cautioned, is finally successful, we shall be less inclined to ridicule his weakness than to be astonished at the infamous ingenuity of a plot which could seduce an understanding so fully prepared. Considerations of worldly interest can have no influence upon my testimony; he, who alone would be thankful for it, is now no more. His dreadful destiny is accomplished; his soul has long since been purified before the throne of truth, where mine will likewise have appeared before these passages meet the eyes of the world. Pardon the involuntary tears which now flow at the remembrance of my dearest friend. But for the sake of justice I must write this. His was a noble character, and would have adorned a throne which, seduced by the most atrocious artifice, he attempted to ascend by the commission of a crime.

BOOK II.

"Not long after these events," continues Count O-----, in his narrative, "I began to observe an extraordinary alteration in the disposition of the prince, which was partly the immediate consequence of the last event and partly produced by the concurrence of many adventitious circumstances. Hitherto he had avoided every severe trial of his faith, and contented himself with purifying the rude and abstract notions of religion, in which he had been educated, by those more rational ideas upon this subject which forced themselves upon his attention, or comparing the many discordant opinions with each other, without inquiring into the foundations of his faith.

Religious subjects, he has many times confessed to me, always appeared to him like an enchanted castle, into which one does not set one's foot without horror, and that they act therefore much the wiser part who pass it in respectful silence, without exposing themselves to the danger of being bewildered in its labyrinths. A servile and bigoted education was the source of this dread; this had impressed frightful images upon his tender brain, which, during the remainder of his life, he was never able wholly to obliterate. Religious melancholy was an hereditary disorder in his family.

The education which he and his brothers had received was calculated to produce it; and the men to whose care they were entrusted, selected with this object, were also either enthusiasts or hypocrites.

"To stifle all the sprightliness of the boy, by a gloomy restraint of his mental faculties, was the only method of securing to themselves the highest approbation of his royal parents. The whole of our prince's childhood wore a dark and gloomy aspect; mirth was banished even from his amusements. All his ideas of religion were accompanied by some frightful image; and the representations of terror and severity were those which first took hold of his lively imagination, and which the longest retained their empire over it. His God was an object of terror, a being whose occupation is to chastise; and the adoration he paid him was either slavish fear, or a blind submission which stifled all his energies. In all his youthful propensities, which a vigorous growth and a fine constitution naturally excited to break out with the greater violence, religion stood in his way; it opposed everything upon which his young heart was bent; he learned to consider it not as a friend, but as the scourge of his passions; so that a silent indignation was gradually kindled against it in his heart, which, together with a bigoted faith and a blind fear, produced an incongruous mixture of feelings, and an abhorrence of a ruler before whom he trembled.

"It is no wonder, therefore, that he took the first opportunity of escaping from so galling a yoke--but he fled from it as a bond-slave who, escaping from his rigorous master, drags along with him a sense of his servitude, even in the midst of freedom; for, as he did not renounce the faith of his earlier years from a deliberate conviction, and did not wait till the maturity and improvement of his reasoning had weaned him from it, but escaped from it like a fugitive, upon whose person the rights of his master are still in force, so was he obliged, even after his widest separation, to return to it at last. He had escaped with his chain, and for that reason must necessarily become the prey of any one who should discover it, and know how to make use of the discovery. That such a one presented himself, the sequel of this history will prove; most likely the reader has already surmised it.

"The confessions of the Sicilian left a deeper impression upon his mind than they ought, considering the circumstances; and the small victory which his reason had thence gained over this weak imposture, remarkably increased his reliance upon his own powers. The facility with which he had been able to unravel this deception appeared to have surprised him. Truth and error were not yet so accurately distinguished from each other in his mind but that he often mistook the arguments which were in favor of the one for those in favor of the other. Thence it arose that the same blow which destroyed his faith in wonders made the whole edifice of it totter. In this instance, he fell into the same error as an inexperienced man who has been deceived in love or friendship, because he happened to make a bad choice, and who denies the existence of these sensations, because he takes the occasional exceptions for distinguishing features. The unmasking of a deception made even truth suspicious to him, because he had unfortunately discovered truth by false reasoning.

"This imaginary triumph pleased him in proportion to the magnitude of the oppression from which it seemed to deliver him. From this instant there arose in his mind a scepticism which did not spare even the most sacred objects.

"Many circumstances concurred to encourage, and still more to confirm, him in this turn of mind. He now quitted the retirement in which he had hitherto lived, and gave way to a more dissipated mode of life. His rank was discovered; attentions which he was obliged to return, etiquettes for which he was indebted to his rank, drew him imperceptibly within the vortex of the great world. His rank, as well as his personal attractions, opened to him the circles of all the beaux esprits in Venice, and he soon found himself on terms of intimacy with the most enlightened persons in the republic, men of learning as well as politicians. This obliged him to en large the monotonous and limited circle to which his understanding had hitherto been confined. He began to perceive the poverty and feebleness of his ideas, and to feel the want of more elevated impressions. The old-fashioned turn of his understanding, in spite of the many advantages with which it was accompanied, formed an unpleasing contrast with the current ideas of society; his ignorance of the commonest things frequently exposed him to ridicule, than which he dreaded nothing more. The unfortunate prejudice which attached to his native country appeared to him a challenge to overcome it in his own person. Besides this, there was a peculiarity in his character; he was offended with every attention that he thought was paid him on account of his rank rather than his personal qualities. He felt this humiliation principally in the company of persons who shone by their abilities, and triumphed, as it were, over their birth by their merit. To perceive himself distinguished as a prince, in such a society, was always a deep humiliation to him, because he unfortunately fancied himself excluded by his rank from all competition. These circumstances convinced him of the necessity of cultivating his mind, in order to raise it to a level with the thinking part of the world, from which he had hitherto been so separated; and for that purpose he chose the most modern books, and applied himself to them with all the ardor with which he was accustomed to pursue every object to which he devoted himself. But the unskilful hand that directed his choice always prompted him to select such as were little calculated to improve either his heart or his reason; besides that, he was influenced by a propensity which rendered everything irresistible which was incomprehensible. He had neither attention nor memory for anything that was not of that character, and both his reason and his heart remained untouched, while he was filling the vacuities of his brain with confused ideas. The dazzling style of some writers captivated his imagination, while the subtlety of others ensnared his reason. Together, they easily took possession of a mind which became the prey of whatever was obtruded upon it with a certain degree of dogmatism. A course of reading, which had been continued with ardor for more than a year, had scarcely enriched him with one benevolent idea, but had filled his head with doubts, which, as a natural consequence with such a character, had almost found an unfortunate road to his heart. In a word, he had entered this labyrinth as a credulous enthusiast, had left it as a sceptic, and at length became a perfect free-thinker.

"Among the circles into which he had been introduced there was a private society called the Bucentauro, which, under the mask of a noble and rational liberality of sentiment, encouraged the most unbridled licentiousness of manners and opinion. As it enumerated many of the clergy among its members, and could even boast of some cardinals at its head, the prince was the more easily induced to join it. He thought that certain dangerous truths, which reason discovers, could be nowhere better preserved than in the hands of such persons, whose rank compelled them to moderation, and who had the advantage of hearing and examining the other side of the question. The prince did not recollect that licentiousness of sentiment and manners takes so much the stronger hold among persons of this rank, inasmuch as they for that reason feel one curb less; and this was the case with the Bucentauro, most of whose members, through an execrable philosophy, and manners worthy of such a guide, were not only a disgrace to their own rank, but even to human nature itself. The society had its secret degrees; and I will believe, for the credit of the prince, that they never thought him worthy of admission into the inmost sanctuary. Every one who entered this society was obliged, at least so long as he continued to be a member of it, to lay aside all distinctions arising from rank, nation, or religion, in short, every general mark or distinction whatever, and to submit himself to the condition of universal equality. To be elected a member was indeed a difficult matter, as superiority of understanding alone paved the way to it. The society boasted of the highest ton and the most cultivated taste, and such indeed was its fame throughout all Venice. This, as well as the appearance of equality which predominated in it, attracted the prince irresistibly. Sensible conversations, set off by the most admirable humor, instructive amusements, and the flower of the learned and political world, which were all attracted to this point as to their common centre, concealed from him for a long time the danger of this connection. As he by degrees discovered through its mask the spirit of the institution, as they grew tired of being any longer on their guard before him, to recede was dangerous, and false shame and anxiety for his safety obliged him to conceal the displeasure he felt. But he already began, merely from familiarity with men of this class and their sentiments, though they did not excite him to imitation, to lose the pure and charming simplicity of his character, and the delicacy of his moral feelings. His understanding, supported by real knowledge, could not without foreign assistance solve the fallacious sophisms with which he had been here ensnared; and this fatal poison had already destroyed all, or nearly all, the basis on which his morality rested.

He surrendered the natural and indispensable safeguards of his happiness for sophisms which deserted him at the critical moment, and he was consequently left to the operation of any specious argument which came in his way.

"Perhaps the hand of a friend might yet have been in time to extricate him from this abyss; but, besides that I did not become acquainted with the real character of the Bucentauro till long after the evil had taken place, an urgent circumstance called me away from Venice just at the beginning of this period. Lord Seymour, too, a valuable acquaintance of the prince, whose cool understanding was proof against every species of deception, and who would have infallibly been a secure support to him, left us at this time in order to return to his native country. Those in whose hands I left the prince were indeed worthy men, but inexperienced, excessively narrow in their religious opinions, deficient in their perception of the evil, and wanting in credit with the prince. They had nothing to oppose to his captious sophisms except the maxims of a blind and uninquiring faith, which either irritated him or excited his ridicule. He saw through them too easily, and his superior reason soon silenced those weak defenders of the good cause, as will be clearly evinced from an instance which I shall introduce in the sequel. Those who, subsequent to this, possessed themselves of his confidence, were much more interested in plunging him deeper into error. When I returned to Venice in the following year how great a change had already taken place in everything!

"The influence of this new philosophy soon showed itself in the prince's conduct. The more openly he pursued pleasure, and acquired new friends, the more did he lose in the estimation of his old ones. He pleased me less and less every day; we saw each other more seldom, and indeed he was seldom accessible. He had launched out into the torrent of the great world. His threshold was eternally thronged when he was at home. Amusements, banquets, and galas followed each other in rapid succession. He was the idol whom every one courted, the great attraction of every circle. In proportion as he, in his secluded life, had fancied living in society to be difficult, did he to his astonishment find it easy. Everything met his wishes. Whatever he uttered was admirable, and when he remained silent it was like committing a robbery upon the company. They understood the art of drawing his thoughts insensibly from his soul, and then with a little delicate management to surprise him with them. This happiness, which accompanied him everywhere, and this universal success, raised him indeed too much in his own ideas, because it gave him too much confidence and too much reliance upon himself.

"The heightened opinion which he thus acquired of his own worth made him credit the excessive and almost idolatrous adoration that was paid to his understanding; which but for this increased self-complacency, must have necessarily recalled him from his aberrations. For the present, however, this universal voice was only a confirmation of what his complacent vanity whispered in his ear; a tribute which he felt entitled to by right. He would have infallibly disengaged himself from this snare had they allowed him to take breath; had they granted him a moment of uninterrupted leisure to compare his real merit with the picture that was exhibited to him in this seducing mirror; but his existence was a continued state of intoxication, a whirl of excitement. The higher he had been elevated the more difficulty had he to support himself in his elevation. This incessant exertion slowly undermined him; rest had forsaken even his slumbers. His weakness had been discovered, and the passion kindled in his breast turned to good account.

"His worthy attendants soon found to their cost that their lord had become a wit. That anxious sensibility, those glorious truths which his heart once embraced with the greatest enthusiasm, now began to be the objects of his ridicule. He revenged himself on the great truths of religion for the oppression which he had so long suffered from misconception. But, since from too true a voice his heart combated the intoxication of his head, there was more of acrimony than of humor in his jests. His disposition began to alter, and caprice to exhibit itself. The most beautiful ornament of his character, his modesty, vanished; parasites had poisoned his excellent heart. That tender delicacy of address which frequently made his attendants forget that he was their lord, now gave place to a decisive and despotic tone, which made the more sensible impression, because it was not founded upon distinction of rank, for the want of which they could have consoled themselves, but upon an arrogant estimation of his own superior merit.

When at home he was attacked by reflections that seldom made their appearance in the bustle of company; his own people scarcely ever saw him otherwise than gloomy, peevish, and unhappy, whilst elsewhere a forced vivacity made him the soul of every circle. With the sincerest sorrow did we behold him treading this dangerous path, but in the vortex in which he was involved the feeble voice of friendship was no longer heard, and he was too much intoxicated to understand it.

"Just at the beginning of this epoch an affair of the greatest consequence required my presence in the court of my sovereign, which I dared not postpone even for the dearest interests of friendship. An invisible hand, the agency of which I did not discover till long afterwards, had contrived to derange my affairs, and to spread reports concerning me which I was obliged to contradict by my presence. The parting from the prince was painful to me, but did not affect him. The ties which united us had been severed for some time, but his fate had awakened all my anxiety. I, on that account, prevailed on Baron von F------ to inform me by letter of every event, which he has done in the most conscientious manner. As I was for a considerable time no longer an eye-witness of these events, it will be allowable for me to introduce the Baron von F------ in my stead, and to fill up the gap in my narrative by the contents of his letters. Notwithstanding that the representation of my friend F------ is not always what I should have given, I would not alter any of his expressions, so that the reader will be enabled to discover the truth with very little trouble."

LETTER I.

BARON VON F TO COUNT VON O.

May 17.

I thank you, my most honored friend, for the permission you have given me to continue in your absence that confidential intercourse with you, which during your stay here formed my great pleasure. You must be aware that there is no one here with whom I can venture to open my heart on certain private matters. Whatever you may urge to the contrary, I detest the people here. Since the prince has become one of them, and since we have lost your society, I feel solitary in the midst of this populous city. Z------ takes it less to heart, and the fair ones of Venice manage to make him forget the mortifications he is compelled to share with me at home. And why should he make himself unhappy? He desires nothing more in the prince than a master, whom he could also find elsewhere. But I!--you know how deep an interest I feel in our prince's weal and woe, and how much cause I have for doing so; I have now lived with him sixteen years, and seem to exist only for his sake. As a boy of nine years old I first entered his service, and since that time we have never been separated. I have grown up under his eye--a long intercourse has insensibly attached me more and more to him--I have borne a part in all his adventures, great and small. Until this last unhappy year I had been accustomed to look upon him in the light of a friend, or of an elder brother--I have basked in his smile as in the sunshine of a summer's day--no cloud hung over my happiness!--and all this must now go to ruin in this unlucky Venice!

Since your departure several changes have taken place in our establishment. The Prince of --d----- arrived here last week, with a numerous and brilliant retinue, and has caused a new and tumultuous life in our circle. As he is so nearly related to our prince, and as they are moreover at present upon pretty good terms, they will be very little apart during his sojourn, which I hear is to last until after the feast of the Ascension. A good beginning has already been made; for the last ten days our prince has hardly had time to breathe.

The Prince of --d---- has all along been living in a very expensive way, which was excusable in him, as he will soon take his departure; but the worst of the business is that he has inoculated our prince with his extravagance, because he could not well withdraw himself from his company, and, in the peculiar relation which exists between the two houses, thought it incumbent upon himself to assert the dignity of his own. We shall, moreover, depart from Venice in a few weeks, which will relieve the prince from the necessity of continuing for any length of time this extraordinary expenditure.

The Prince of --d-----, it is reported, is here on business of the Order, in which he imagines that he plays an important part. That he has taken advantage of all the acquaintances of our prince you may readily imagine. He has been introduced with distinguished honor into the society of the Bucentauro, as he is pleased to consider himself a wit, and a man of great genius, and allows himself to be styled in his correspondences, which he keeps up throughout all parts of the world, the "prince philosophique." I do not know whether you have ever had the pleasure of meeting him. He displays a promising exterior, piercing eyes, a countenance full of expression, much show of reading, much acquired naturalness (if I may be allowed the expression), joined to a princely condescension towards the human race, a large amount of confidence in himself, and an eloquence which talks down all opposition. Who could refuse to pay homage to such splendid qualities in a "Royal Highness?" But to what advantage the quiet and sterling worth of our prince will appear, when contrasted with these dazzling accomplishments, the event must show.

In the arrangement of our establishment, various and important changes have taken place. We have rented a new and magnificent house opposite the new Procuracy, because the lodging at the Moor Hotel became too confined for the prince. Our suite has been augmented by twelve persons, pages, Moors, guards, etc. During your stay here you complained of unnecessary expense--you should see us now!

Our internal arrangements remain the same as of old, except that the prince, no longer held in check by your presence, is, if possible, more reserved and distant towards us than ever; we see very little of him, except while dressing or undressing him. Under the pretext that we speak the French language very badly, and the Italian not at all, he has found means to exclude us from most of his entertainments, which to me personally is not a very great grievance; but I believe I know the true reason of it--he is ashamed of us; and this hurts me, for we have not deserved it of him.

As you wish to know all our minor affairs, I must tell you, that of all his attendants, the prince almost exclusively employs Biondello, whom he took into his service, as you will recollect, on the disappearance of his huntsman, and who, in his new mode of life, has become quite indispensable to him.

This man knows Venice thoroughly, and turns everything to some account. It is as though he had a thousand eyes, and could set a thousand hands in motion at once. This he accomplishes, as he says, by the help of the gondoliers. To the prince he renders himself very useful by making him acquainted with all the strange faces that present themselves at his assemblies, and the private information he gives his highness has always proved to be correct. Besides this, he speaks and writes both Italian and French excellently, and has in consequence already risen to be the prince's secretary. I must, however, relate to you an instance of fidelity in him which is rarely found among people of his station. The other day a merchant of good standing from Rimini requested an audience of the prince. The object of his visit was an extraordinary complaint concerning Biondello. The procurator, his former master, who must have been rather an odd fellow, had lived in irreconcilable enmity with his relations; this enmity he wished if possible to continue even after his death. Biondello possessed his entire confidence, and was the repository of all his secrets; while on his deathbed he obliged him to swear that he would keep them inviolably, and would never disclose them for the benefit of his relations; a handsome legacy was to be the reward of his silence. When the deceased procurator's will was opened and his papers inspected, many blanks and irregularities were found to which Biondello alone could furnish a key. He persisted in denying that he knew anything about it, gave up his very handsome legacy to the heirs, and kept his secrets to himself. Large offers were made to him by the relations, but all in vain; at length, in order to escape from their importunities and their threats of legally prosecuting him he entered the service of the prince. The merchant, who was the chief heir, now applied to the prince, and made larger offers than, before if Biondello would alter his determination. But even the persuasions of the prince were fruitless. He admitted that secrets of consequence had really been confided to him; he did not deny that the deceased had perhaps carried his enmity towards his relations too far; but, added he, he was my dear master and benefactor, and died with a firm belief in my integrity. I was the only friend he had left in the world, and will therefore never prove myself unworthy of his confidence. At the same time he hinted that the avowals they wished him to make would not tend to the honor of the deceased. Was not that acting nobly and delicately? You may easily imagine that the prince did not renew his endeavors to shake so praiseworthy a determination. The extraordinary fidelity which he has shown towards his deceased master has procured him the unlimited confidence of his present one!

Farewell, my dear friend. How I sigh for the quiet life we led when first you came amongst us, for the stillness of which your society so agreeably indemnified us. I fear my happy days in Venice are over, and shall be glad if the same remark does not also apply to the prince. The element in which he now lives is not calculated to render him permanently happy, or my sixteen years' experience has deceived me.

LETTER II.

BARON VON F TO COUNT VON O. June 4.

    I should never have thought that our stay at Venice would have been productive of any good consequences. It has been the means of saving a man's life, and I am reconciled to it.

    Some few evenings ago the prince was being carried home late at night from the Bucentauro; two domestics, of whom Biondello was one, accompanied him. By some accident it happened that the sedan, which had been hired in haste, broke down, and the prince was obliged to proceed the remainder of the way-on foot. Biondello walked in front; their course lay through several dark, retired streets, and, as daybreak was at hand, the lamps were either burning dimly or had gone out altogether. They had proceeded about a quarter of an hour when Biondello discovered that he had lost his way. The similarity of the bridges had deceived him, and, instead of crossing that of St. Mark, they found themselves in Sestiere di Castello. It was in a by-street, and not a soul was stirring; they were obliged to turn back in order to gain a main street by which to set themselves right. They had proceeded but a few paces when they heard cries of "murder" in a neighboring street. With his usual determined courage, the prince, unarmed as he was, snatched a stick from one of his attendants, and rushed forward in the direction whence the sound came. Three ruffianly-looking fellows were just about to assassinate a man, who with his companion was feebly defending himself; the prince appeared just in time to arrest the fatal blow. The voices of the prince and his followers alarmed the murderers, who did not expect any interruption in so lonely a place; after inflicting a few slight wounds with their daggers, they abandoned their victim and took to their heels. Exhausted with the unequal combat, the wounded man sunk half fainting into the arms of the prince; his companion informed my master that the man whose life he had saved was the Marquis Civitella, a nephew of the Cardinal A------. As the marquis' wounds bled freely, Biondello acted as surgeon to the best of his ability, and the prince took care to have him conveyed to the palace of his uncle, which was near at hand, and whither he himself accompanied him. This done, he left the house without revealing his name.

This, however, was discovered by a servant who had recognized Biondello. Already on the following morning the cardinal, an old acquaintance from the Bucentauro, waited upon the prince. The interview lasted an hour; the cardinal was much moved; tears stood in his eyes when they parted; the prince, too, was affected. The same evening a visit was paid to the sick man, of whose case the surgeon gives a very favorable report; the mantle in which he was wrapped had rendered the thrusts unsteady, and weakened their force. Since this event not a day has passed without the prince's paying a visit at the cardinal's, or receiving one from him, and a close intimacy has begun to exist between him and the cardinal's family.

The cardinal is a venerable man of sixty, with a majestic aspect, but full of gayety and good health. He is said to be the richest prelate throughout all the dominions of the republic. He is reported to manage his immense fortune in a very liberal manner, and, although prudently economical, to despise none of the joys of this life. This nephew, who is his sole heir, is not always on the best of terms with his uncle. For, although the cardinal is anything but an enemy to youthful pleasures, the conduct of the nephew must exhaust the utmost tolerance. His loose principles and dissipated manner of living, aided unhappily by all the attractions which can make vice tempting and excite sensuality, have rendered him the terror of all fathers and the bane of all husbands; this last attack also was said to have been caused by an intrigue he had begun with the wife of the ambassador, without speaking of other serious broils from which the power and the money of the cardinal could scarcely extricate him. But for this the cardinal would be the happiest man in Italy, for he possesses everything that can make life agreeable; but by this one domestic misfortune all the gifts of fortune are annulled, and the enjoyment of his wealth is embittered to the cardinal by the continual fear of finding nobody to inherit it.

The whole of this information I have obtained from Biondello. The prince has found in this man a real treasure. Every day he becomes more indispensable, and we are continually discovering in him some new talent. Some days ago the prince felt feverish and could not sleep; the night-lamp was extinguished, and all his ringing failed to arouse the valet-de-chambre, who had gone to sleep out of the house with an opera-dancer. At length the prince determined to rise himself, and to rouse one of his people. He had not proceeded far when a strain of delicious melody met his ear. Like one enchanted, he followed the sound, and found Biondello in his room playing upon the flute, with his fellow-servants assembled around him. The prince could hardly believe his senses, and commanded him to proceed. With a surprising degree of facility he began to vary a touching adagio air with some fine extempore variations, which he executed with all the taste of a virtuoso. The prince, who, as you know, is a judge of music, says that he might play with confidence in the finest choir in Italy.

"I must dismiss this man," said he to me next morning, "for I am unable to reward him according to his merits." Biondello, who had overheard these words, came forward, "If you dismiss me, gracious prince," said he, "you deprive me of my best reward."

"You are born to something better than to serve," answered my master. "I must not stand in the way of your fortune."

"Do not press upon me any better fortune, gracious sir, than that which I have chosen for myself."

"To neglect talent like yours--No! I can never permit it."

"Then permit me, gracious sir, sometimes to exercise it in your presence."

Preparations were immediately made for carrying this proposition into effect. Biondello had a room assigned to him next the apartment of the prince, so that he can lull him to sleep with his strains, and wake him in the same manner. The prince wished to double his salary, but Biondello declined, requesting that this intended boon should be retained in his master's hands as a capital of which he might some day wish to avail himself. The prince expects that he will soon come to ask a favor at his hands; and whatever it may be it is granted beforehand. Farewell, dearest friend. I am waiting with impatience for tidings from K-----n.

LETTER III.

BARON VON F TO COUNT VON O June 4.

The Marquis of Civitella, who is now entirely recovered from his wounds, was last week introduced to the prince by his uncle, the cardinal, and since then he has followed him like his shadow. Biondello cannot have told me the truth respecting this marquis, or at any rate his account must be greatly exaggerated. His mien is highly engaging, and his manners irresistibly winning.

It is impossible to be out of humor with him; the first sight of him has disarmed me. Imagine a man of the most enchanting figure, with corresponding grace and dignity, a countenance full of thought and genius, an expression frank and inviting; a persuasive tone of voice, the most flowing eloquence, and a glow of youthful beauty, joined to all theadvantages of a most liberal education. He has none of that contemptuous pride, none of that solemn starchness, which we disliked so much in all the other nobles. His whole being is redolent of youthful joyousness, benevolence, and warmth of feeling. His excesses must have been much exaggerated; I never saw a more perfect picture of health. If he is really so wholly abandoned as Biondello represents him he is a syren whom none can resist.

Towards me he behaved with much frankness. He confessed with the most pleasing sincerity that he was by no means on the best of terms with his uncle, the cardinal, and that it was his own fault. But he was seriously resolved to amend his life, and the merit would be entirely the prince's. At the same time he hoped through his instrumentality to be reconciled to his uncle, as the prince's influence with the cardinal was unbounded. The only thing he had wanted till now was a friend and a guide, and he trusted he should find both in the person of the prince.

The prince has now assumed the authority of a preceptor towards him, and treats him with all the watchfulness fulness and strictness of a Mentor. But this intimacy also gives the marquis a certain degree of influence, of which he well knows how to avail himself. He hardly stirs from his side; he is present at all parties where the prince is one of the guests; for the Bucentauro alone he is fortunately as yet too young. Wherever be appears in public with the prince he manages to draw him away from the rest of the company by the pleasing manner in which he engages him in conversation and arrests his attention. Nobody, they say, has yet been able to reclaim him, and the prince will deserve to be immortalized in an epic should he accomplish such an Herculean task. I am much afraid, however, that the tables may be turned, and the guide be led away by the pupil, of which, in fact, there seems to be every prospect.

The Prince of ---d------ has taken his departure, much to the satisfaction of us all, my master not excepted. What I predicted, my dear O-----, has come to pass. Two characters so widely opposed must inevitably clash together, and cannot maintain a good understanding for any length of time. The Prince of ---d------ had not been long in Venice before a terrible schism took place in the intellectual world, which threatened to deprive our prince of one-half of his admirers. Wherever he went he was crossed by this rival, who possessed exactly the requisite amount of small cunning to avail himself of every little advantage he gained. As he besides never scrupled to make use of any petty manoeuvres to increase his consequence, he in a short time drew all the weak-minded of the community on his side, and shone at the head of a company of parasites worthy of such a leader.

[The harsh judgment which Baron F----- (both here and in some passages of his first letter) pronounces upon this talented prince will be found exaggerated by every one who has the good fortune to be acquainted with him, and must be attributed to the prejudiced views of the young observer.--Note of the Count von O------.]

The wiser course would certainly have been not to enter into competition at all with an adversary of this description, and a few months back this is the part which the prince would have taken. But now he has launched too far into the stream easily to regain the shore. These trifles have, perhaps by the circumstances in which he is placed, acquired a certain degree of importance in his eyes, and had he even despised them his pride would not have allowed him to retire at a moment when his yielding would have been looked upon less as a voluntary act than as a confession of inferiority.

Added to this, an unlucky revival of forgotten satirical speeches had taken place, and the spirit of rivalry which took possession of his followers had affected the prince himself. In order, therefore, to maintain that position in society which public opinion had now assigned him, he deemed it advisable to seize every possible opportunity of display, and of increasing the number of his admirers; but this could only be effected by the most princely expenditure; he was therefore eternally giving feasts, entertainments, and expensive concerts, making costly presents, and playing high. As this strange madness, moreover, had also infected the prince's retinue, who are generally much more punctilious in respect to what they deem "the honor of the family" than their masters, the prince was obliged to assist the zeal of his followers by his liberality. Here, then, is a whole catalogue of ills, all irremediable consequences of a sufficiently excusable weakness to which the prince in an unguarded moment gave way.

We have, it is true, got rid of our rival, but the harm he has done will not so soon be remedied. The finances of the prince are exhausted; all that he had saved by the wise economy of years is spent; and he must hasten from Venice if he would escape plunging into debt, which till now he has most scrupulously avoided. It is decisively settled that we leave as soon as fresh remittances arrive.

I should not have minded all this splendor if the prince had but reaped the least real satisfaction from it. But he was never less happy than at present.

He feels that he is not what he formerly was; he seeks to regain his self-respect; he is dissatisfied with himself, and launches into fresh dissipation in order to drown the recollection of the last. One new acquaintance follows another, and each involves him more deeply. I know not where this will end. We must away--there is no other chance of safety--we must away from Venice.

But, my dear friend, I have not yet received a single line from you. How am I to interpret this long and obstinate silence?

LETTER IV.

BARON VON F------ TO COUNT VON O------. June 12.

I thank you, my dear friend, for the token of your remembrance which young B---hl brought me. But what is it you say about letters I ought to have received? I have received no letter from you; not a single one. What a circuitous route must they have taken. In future, dear O------, when you honor me with an epistle despatch it via Trent, under cover to the prince, my master.

We have at length been compelled, my dear friend, to resort to a measure which till now we had so happily avoided. Our remittances have failed to arrive--failed, for the first time, in this pressing emergency, and we have been obliged to have recourse to a usurer, as the prince is willing to pay handsomely to keep the affair secret. The worst of this disagreeable occurrence is, that it retards our departure. On this affair the prince and I have had an explanation. The whole transaction had been arranged by Biondello, and the son of Israel was there before I had any suspicion of the fact. It grieved me to the heart to see the prince reduced to such an extremity, and revived all my recollections of the past, and fears for the future; and I suppose I may have looked rather sorrowful and gloomy when the usurer left the room. The prince, whom the foregoing scene had left in not the happiest frame of mind, was pacing angrily up and down the room; the rouleaus of gold were still lying on the table; I stood at the window, counting the panes of glass in the procurator's house opposite. There was a long pause. At length the prince broke silence. "F------!" he began, "I cannot bear to see dismal faces about me."

I remained silent.

"Why do you not answer me? Do I not perceive that your heart is almost bursting to vent some of its vexation? I insist on your speaking, otherwise you will begin to fancy that you are keeping some terribly momentous secret."

"If I am gloomy, gracious sir," replied I, "it is only because I do not see you cheerful."

"I know," continued he, "that you have been dissatisfied with me for some time past--that you disapprove of every step I take--that--what does Count O------ say in his letters?"

"Count O------ has not written to me."

"Not written? Why do you deny it? You keep up a confidential correspondence together, you and the count; I am quite aware of that. Come, you may confess it, for I have no wish to pry into your secrets."

"Count O------," replied I, "has not yet answered any of the three letters which I have written to him."

"I have done wrong," continued he; "don't you think so?" (taking up one of the rouleaus) "I should not have done this?"

"I see that it was necessary."

"I ought not to have reduced myself to such a necessity?" I did not answer.

"Oh, of course! I ought never to have indulged my wishes, but have grown gray in the same dull manner in which I was brought up! Because I once venture a step beyond the drear monotony of my past life, and look around me to see whether there be not some new source of enjoyment in store for me--because I--"

"If it was but a trial, gracious sir, I have no more to say; for the experience you have gained would not be dearly bought at three times the price it has cost. It grieves me, I confess, to think that the opinion of the world should be concerned in determining the question--how are you to choose your own happiness."

"It is well for you that you can afford to despise the world's opinion," replied he, "I am its creature, I must be its slave. What are we princes but opinion? With us it is everything. Public opinion is our nurse and preceptor in infancy, our oracle and idol in riper years, our staff in old age. Take from us what we derive from the opinion of the world, and the poorest of the humblest class is in a better position than we, for his fate has taught him a lesson of philosophy which enables him to bear it. But a prince who laughs at the world's opinion destroys himself, like the priest who denies the existence of a God."

"And yet, gracious prince--"

"I see what you would say; I can break through the circle which my birth has drawn around me. But can I also eradicate from my memory all the false impressions which education and early habit have implanted, and which a hundred thousand fools have been continually laboring to impress more and more firmly? Everybody naturally wishes to be what he is in perfection; in short, the whole aim of a prince's existence is to appear happy. If we cannot be happy after your fashion, is that any reason why we should discard all other means of happiness, and not be happy at all? If we cannot drink of joy pure from the fountain-head, can there be any reason why we should not beguile ourselves with artificial pleasure-- nay, even be content to accept a sorry substitute from the very hand that robs us of the higher boon?"

"You were wont to look for this compensation in your own heart."

"But if I no longer find it there? Oh, how came we to fall on this subject? Why did you revive these recollections in me? I had recourse to this tumult of the senses in order to stifle an inward voice which embitters my whole life; in order to lull to rest this inquisitive reason, which, like a sharp sickle, moves to and fro in my brain, at each new research lopping off another branch of my happiness."

"My dearest prince"--He had risen, and was pacing up and down the room in unusual agitation.

[I have endeavored, dearest O------, to relate to you this remarkable conversation exactly as it occurred; but this I found impossible, although I sat down to write it the evening of the day it took place. In order to assist my memory I was obliged to transpose the observation of the prince, and thus this compound of a conversation and a philosophical lecture, which is in some respects better and in others worse than the source from which I took it, arose; but I assure you that I have rather omitted some of the prince's words than ascribed to him any of my own; all that is mine is the arrangement, and a few observations, whose ownership you will easily recognize by their stupidity.-- Note of the Baron von F------]

"When everything gives way before me and behind me; when the past lies in the distance in dreary monotony, like a city of the dead; when the future offers me naught; when I see my whole being enclosed within the narrow circle of the present, who can blame me if I clasp this niggardly present of time in my arms with fiery eagerness, as though it were a friend whom I was embracing for the last time? Oh, I have learnt to value the present moment. The present moment is our mother; let us love it as such."

"Gracious sir, you were wont to believe in a more lasting good."

"Do but make the enchantment last and fervently will I embrace it. But what pleasure can it give to me to render beings happy who to-morrow will have passed away like myself? Is not everything passing away around me? Each one bustles and pushes his neighbor aside hastily to catch a few drops from the fountain of life, and then departs thirsting. At this very moment, while I am rejoicing in lily strength, some being is waiting to start into life at my dissolution. Show me one being who will endure, and I will become a virtuous man."

"But what, then, has become of those benevolent sentiments which used to be the joy and the rule of your life? To sow seeds for the future, to assist in carrying out the designs of a high and eternal Providence"--

"Future! Eternal Providence! If you take away from man all that he derives from his own heart, all that he associates with the idea of a godhead, and all that belongs to the law of nature, what, then, do you leave him?

"What has already happened to me, and what may still follow, I look upon as two black, impenetrable curtains hanging over the two extremities of human life, and which no mortal has ever yet drawn aside. Many hundred generations have stood before the second of these curtains, casting the light of their torches upon its folds, speculating and guessing as to what it may conceal. Many have beheld themselves, in the magnified image of their passions, reflected upon the curtain which hides futurity from their gaze, and have turned away shuddering from their own shadows. Poets, philosophers, and statesmen have painted their fancies on the curtain in brighter or more sombre colors, according as their own prospects were bright or gloomy. Many a juggler has also taken advantage of the universal curiosity, and by well-managed deceptions led astray the excited imagination. A deep silence reigns behind this curtain; no one who passes beyond it answers any questions; all the reply is an empty echo, like the sound yielded by a vault.

"Sooner or later all must go behind this curtain, and they approach it with fear and trembling, in doubt who may be waiting there behind to receive them; quid sit id, quod tantum morituri vident. There have been infidels who asserted that this curtain only deluded mankind, and that we saw nothing behind it, because there was nothing there to see; but, to convince them, they were quickly sent behind it themselves."

"It was indeed a rash conclusion," said I, "if they had no better ground for it than that they saw nothing themselves."

"You see, my dear friend, I am modest enough not to wish to look behind this curtain, and the wisest course will doubtless be to abstain from all curiosity. But while I draw this impassable circle around me, and confine myself within the bounds of present existence, this small point of time, which I was in danger of neglecting in useless researches, becomes the more important to me. What you call the chief end and aim of my existence concerns me no longer. I cannot escape my destiny; I cannot promote its consummation; but I know, and firmly believe, that I am here to accomplish some end, and that I do accomplish it. But the means which nature has chosen to fulfil my destiny are so much the more sacred to me; to me it is everything; my morality, my happiness. All the rest I shall never learn. I am like a messenger who carries a sealed letter to its place of destination. What the letter contains is indifferent to him; his business is only to earn his fee for carrying it."

"Alas!" said I, "how poor a thing you would leave me!"

"But in what a labyrinth have we lost ourselves!" exclaimed the prince, looking with a smile at the table on which the rouleaus lay. "After all perhaps not far from the mark," continued he; "you will now no doubt understand my reasons for this new mode of life. I could not so suddenly tear myself away from my fancied wealth, could not so readily separate the props of my morality and happiness from the pleasing dream with which everything within me was so closely bound up. I longed for the frivolity which seems to render the existence of most of those about me endurable to themselves. Everything which precluded reflection was welcome to me.

Shall I confess it to you? I wished to lower myself, in order to destroy this source of my griefs, by deadening the power of reflection."

Here we were interrupted by a visit. In my next I shall have to communicate to you a piece of news, which, from the tenor of a conversation like the one of to-day, you would scarcely have anticipated.

LETTER V.

BARON VON F------ TO COUNT VON O------.

As the time of our departure from Venice is now approaching with rapid steps, this week was to be devoted to seeing everything worthy of notice in pictures and public edifices; a task which, when one intends making a long stay in a place, is always delayed till the last moment.

The "Marriage at Cana," by Paul Veronese, which is to be seen in a Benedictine convent in the Island of St. George, was in particular mentioned to us in high terms. Do not expect me to give you a description of this extraordinary work of art, which, on the whole, made a very surprising, but not equally pleasing, impression on me. We should have required as many hours as we had minutes to study a composition of one hundred and twenty figures, upon a ground thirty feet broad. What human eye is capable of grasping so complicated a whole, or at once to enjoy all the beauty which the artist has everywhere lavished, upon it! It is, however, to be lamented, that a work of so much merit, which if exhibited in some public place, would command the admiration of every one, should be destined merely to ornament the refectory of a few monks. The church of the monastery is no less worthy of admiration, being one of the finest in the whole city. Towards evening we went in a gondola to the Guidecca, in order to spend the pleasant hours of evening in its charming garden. Our party, which was not very numerous, soon dispersed in various directions; and Civitella, who had been waiting all day for an opportunity of speaking to me privately, took me aside into an arbor.

"You are a friend to the prince," he began, "from whom he is accustomed to keep no secrets, as I know from very good authority. As I entered his hotel to-day I met a man coming out whose occupation is well known to me, and when I entered the room the prince's brow was clouded." I wished to interrupt him,--"You cannot deny it," continued he; "I knew the man, I looked at him well. And is it possible that the prince should have a friend in Venice--a friend who owes his life to him, and yet be reduced on an emergency to make use of such creatures?"

"Tell me frankly, Baron! Is the prince in difficulties? It is in vain you strive to conceal it from me. What! you refuse to tell me! I can easily learn from one who would sell any secret for gold."

"My good Marquis!"

"Pardon me! I must appear intrusive in order not to be ungrateful. To the prince I am indebted for life, and what is still more, for a reasonable use of it. Shall I stand idly by and see him take steps which, besides being inconvenient to him, are beneath his dignity? Shall I feel it in my power to assist him, and hesitate for a moment to step forward?"

"The prince," replied I, "is not in difficulties. Some remittances which we expected via Trent have not yet arrived, most likely either by accident, or because not feeling certain whether he had not already left Venice, they waited for a communication from him. This has now been done, and until their arrival--"

Civitella shook his head. "Do not mistake my motive," said he; "in this there can be no question as to diminishing the extent of my obligations towards the prince, which all my uncle's wealth would be insufficient to cancel. My object is simply to spare him a few unpleasant moments. My uncle possesses a large fortune which I can command as freely as though it were my own. A fortunate circumstance occurs, which enables me to avail myself of the only means by which I can possibly be of the slightest use to your master. I know," continued he, "how much delicacy the prince possesses, but the feeling is mutual, and it would be noble on his part to afford me this slight gratification, were it only to make me appear to feel less heavily the load of obligation under which I labor."

He continued to urge his request, until I had pledged my word to assist him to the utmost of my ability. I knew the prince's character, and had but small hopes of success. The marquis promised to agree to any conditions the prince might impose, but added, that it would deeply wound him to be regarded in the light of a stranger.

In the heat of our conversation we had strayed far away from the rest of the company, and were returning, when Z-------- came to meet us.

"I am in search of the prince," he cried; "is he not with you?"

"We were just going to him," was our reply. "We thought to find him with the rest of the party."

"The company is all together, but he is nowhere to be found. I cannot imagine how we lost sight of him."

It now occurred to Civitella that he might have gone to look at the adjoining church, which had a short time before attracted his attention. We immediately went to look for him there. As we approached, we found Biondello waiting in the porch. On coming nearer, we saw the prince emerge hastily from a side door; his countenance was flushed, and he looked anxiously round for Biondello, whom he called. He seemed to be giving him very particular instructions for the execution of some commission, while his eyes continued constantly fixed on the church door, which had remained open. Biondello hastened into the church. The prince, without perceiving us, passed through the crowd, and went back to his party, which he reached before us.

We resolved to sup in an open pavilion of the garden, where the marquis had, without our knowledge, arranged a little concert, which was quite first-rate. There was a young singer in particular, whose delicious voice and charming figure excited general admiration. Nothing, however, seemed to make an impression on the prince; he spoke little, and gave confused answers to our questions; his eyes were anxiously fixed in the direction whence he expected Biondello; and he seemed much agitated. Civitella asked him what he thought of the church; he was unable to give any description of it. Some beautiful pictures, which rendered the church remarkable, were spoken of; the prince had not noticed them. We perceived that our questions annoyed him, and therefore discontinued them. Hour after hour rolled on and still Biondello returned not. The prince could no longer conceal his impatience; he rose from the table, and paced alone, with rapid strides, up and down a retired walk. Nobody could imagine what had happened to him. I did not venture to ask him the reason of so remarkable a change in his demeanor; I have for some time past resigned my former place in his confidence. It was, therefore, with the utmost impatience that I awaited the return of Biondello to explain this riddle to me.

It was past ten o'clock when he made his appearance. The tidings he brought did not make the prince more communicative. He returned in an illhumor to the company, the gondola was ordered, and we returned. home.

During the remainder of that evening I could find no opportunity of speaking to Biondello, and was, therefore, obliged to retire to my pillow with my curiosity unsatisfied. The prince had dismissed us early, but a thousand reflections flitted across my brain, and kept me awake. For a long time I could hear him pacing up and down his room; at length sleep overcame me. Late at midnight I was awakened by a voice, and I felt a hand passed across my face; I opened my eyes, and saw the prince standing at my bedside, with a lamp in his hand. He told me he was unable to sleep, and begged me to keep him company through the night. I was going to dress myself, but he told me to stay where I was, and seated himself at my bedside.

"Something has happened to me to-day," he began, "the impression of which will never be effaced from my soul. I left you, as you know, to see the church, respecting which Civitella had raised my curiosity, and which had already attracted my attention. As neither you nor he were at hand, I walked the short distance alone, and ordered Biondello to wait for me at the door. The church was quite empty; a dim and solemn light surrounded me as I entered from the blazing sultry day without. I stood alone in the spacious building, throughout which there reigned the stillness of the grave. I placed myself in the centre of the church, and gave myself up to the feelings which the sight was calculated to produce; by degrees the grand proportions of this majestic building expanded to my gaze, and I stood wrapt in deep and pleasing contemplation. Above me the evening bell was tolling; its tones died softly away in the aisles, and found an echo in my heart. Some altar-pieces at a distance attracted my attention. I approached to look at them; unconsciously I had wandered through one side of the church, and was now standing at the opposite end. Here a few steps, raised round a pillar, led into a little chapel, containing several small altars, with statues of saints in the niches above them. On entering the chapel on the right I heard a whispering, as though some one near was speaking in a low voice. I turned towards the spot whence the sound proceeded, and saw before me a female form. No! I cannot describe to you the beauty of this form. My first feeling was one of awe, which, however, soon gave place to ravishing surprise."

"But this figure, your highness? Are you certain that it was something living, something real, and not perhaps a picture, or an illusion of your fancy?"

"Hear me further. It was a lady. Surely, till that moment, I have never seen her sex in its full perfection! All around was sombre; the setting sun shone through a single window into the chapel, and its rays rested upon her figure. With inexpressible grace, half kneeling, half lying, she was stretched before an altar; one of the most striking, most lovely, and picturesque objects in all nature. Her dress was of black moreen, fitting tightly to her slender waist and beautifully-formed arms, the skirts spreading around her like a Spanish robe; her long light-colored hair was divided into two broad plaits, which, apparently from their own weight, had escaped from under her veil, and flowed in charming disorder down her back. One of her hands grasped the crucifix, and her head rested gracefully upon the other. But, where shall I find words to describe to you the angelic beauty of her countenance, in which the charms of a seraph seemed displayed. The setting sun shone full upon her face, and its golden beams seemed to surround it as with a glory. Can you recall to your mind the Madonna of our Florentine painter? She was here personified, even to those few deviations from the studied costume which so powerfully, so irresistibly attracted me in the picture."

With regard to the Madonna, of whom the prince spoke, the case is this: Shortly after your departure he made the acquaintance of a Florentine painter, who had been summoned to Venice to paint an altar-piece for some church, the name of which I do not recollect. He had brought with him three paintings, which had been intended for the gallery in the Cornari palace. They consisted of a Madonna, a Heloise, and a Venus, very lightly apparelled. All three were of great beauty; and, although the subjects were quite different, they were so intrinsically equal that it seemed almost impossible to determine which to prefer. The prince alone did not hesitate for a moment. As soon as the pictures were placed before him the Madonna absorbed his whole attention; in the two others he admired the painter's genius; but in this he forgot the artist and his art, his whole soul being absorbed in the contemplation of the work. He was quite moved, and could scarcely tear himself away from it. We could easily see by the artist's countenance that in his heart he coincided with the prince's judgment; he obstinately refused to separate the pictures, and demanded fifteen hundred zechins for the three. The prince offered him half that sum for the Madonna alone, but in vain. The artist insisted on his first demand, and who knows what might have been the result if a ready purchaser had not stepped forward.

Two hours afterwards all three pictures were sold, and we never saw them again. It was this Madonna which now recurred to the prince's mind.

"I stood," continued he, "gazing at her in silent admiration. She did not observe me; my arrival did not disturb her, so completely was she absorbed in her devotion. She prayed to her Deity, and I prayed to her --yes, I adored her! All the pictures of saints, all the altars and the burning tapers around me had failed to remind me of what now for the first time burst upon me, that I was in a sacred place. Shall I confess it to you? In that moment I believed firmly in Him whose image was clasped in her beautiful hand. I read in her eyes that he answered her prayers. Thanks be to her charming devotion, it had revealed him to me. I wandered with her through all the paradise of prayer.

"She rose, and I recollected myself. I stepped aside confused; but the noise I made in moving discovered me. I thought that the unexpected presence of a man might alarm, that my boldness would offend her; but neither of these feelings were expressed in the look with which she regarded me. Peace, benign peace, was portrayed in her countenance, and a cheerful smile played upon her lips. She was descending from her heaven; and I was the first happy mortal who met her benevolent look. Her mind was still wrapt in her concluding prayer; she had not yet come in contact with earth.

"I now heard something stir in the opposite corner of the chapel. It was an elderly lady, who rose from a cushion close behind me. Till now I had not observed her. She had been distant only a few steps from me. and must have seen my every motion. This confused me. I cast my eyes to the earth, and both the ladies passed by me."

On this last point I thought myself able to console the prince.

"Strange," continued he, after a long silence, "that there should be something which one has never known--never missed; and that yet on a sudden one should seem to live and breathe for that alone. Can one single moment so completely metamorphose a human being? It would now be as impossible for me to indulge in the wishes or enjoy the pleasures of yesterday as it would be to return to the toys of my childhood, and all this since I have seen this object which lives and rules in the inmost recesses of my soul. It seems to say that I can love nothing else, and that nothing else in this world can produce an impression on me."

"But consider, gracious prince," said I, "the excitable mood you were in when this apparition surprised you, and how all the circumstances conspired to inflame your imagination. Quitting the dazzling light of day and the busy throng of men, you were suddenly surrounded by twilight and repose. You confess that you had quite given yourself up to those solemn emotions which the majesty of the place was calculated to awaken; the contemplation of fine works of art had rendered you more susceptible to the impressions of beauty in any form. You supposed yourself alone-- when you saw a maiden who, I will readily allow, may have been very beautiful, and whose charms were heightened by a favorable illumination of the setting sun, a graceful attitude, and an expression of fervent devotion--what is more natural than that your vivid fancy should look upon such a form as something supernaturally perfect?"

"Can the imagination give what it never received?" replied he. "In the whole range of my fancy there is nothing which I can compare with that image. It is impressed on my mind distinctly and vividly as in the moment when I beheld it. I can think of nothing but that picture; but you might offer me whole worlds for it in vain."

"My gracious prince, this is love."

"Must the sensation which makes me happy necessarily have a name? Love! Do not degrade my feeling by giving it a name which is so often misapplied by the weak-minded. Who ever felt before what I do now? Such a being never before existed; how then can the name be admitted before the emotion which it is meant to express? Mine is a novel and peculiar feeling, connected only with this being, and capable of being applied to her alone.

Love! From love I am secure!"

"You sent away Biondello, no doubt, to follow in the steps of these strangers, and to make inquiries concerning them. What news did he bring you?"

"Biondello discovered nothing; or, at least, as good as nothing. An aged, respectably dressed man, who looked more like a citizen than a servant, came to conduct them to their gondola. A number of poor people placed themselves in a row, and quitted her, apparently well satisfied. Biondello said he saw one of her hands, which was ornamented with several precious stones. She spoke a few words, which Biondello could not comprehend, to her companion; he says it was Greek. As she had some distance to walk to the canal, the people began to throng together, attracted by the strangeness of her appearance. Nobody knew her--but beauty seems born to rule. All made way for her in a respectful manner. She let fall a black veil, that covered half of her person, over her face, and hastened into the gondola.

Along the whole Giudecca Biondello managed to keep the boat in view, but the crowd prevented his following it further."

"But surely he took notice of the gondolier so as to be able to recognize him again."

"He has undertaken to find out the gondolier, but he is not one of those with whom he associates. The mendicants, whom he questioned, could give him no further information than that the signora had come to the church for the last few Saturdays, and had each time divided a gold-piece among them. It was a Dutch ducat, which Biondello changed for them, and brought to me."

"It appears, then, that she is a Greek--most likely of rank; at any rate, rich and charitable. That is as much as we dare venture to conclude at present, gracious sir; perhaps too much. But a Greek lady in a Catholic church?"

"Why not? She may have changed her religion. But there is certainly some mystery in the affair. Why should she go only once a week? Why always on Saturday, on which day, as Biondello tells me, the church is generally deserted. Next Saturday, at the latest, must decide this question. Till then, dearest friend, you must help me to while away the hours. But it is in vain. They will go their lingering pace, though my soul is burning with expectation!"

"And when this day at length arrives--what, then, gracious prince? What do you purpose doing?"

"What do I purpose doing? I shall see her. I will discover where she lives and who she is. But to what does all this tend? I hear you ask. What I saw made me happy; I therefore now know wherein my happiness consists!"

"And our departure from Venice, which is fixed for next Monday?"

"How could I know that Venice still contained such a treasure for me? You ask me questions of my past life. I tell you that from this day forward I will begin a new existence."

I thought that now was the opportunity to keep my word to the marquis. I explained to the prince that a protracted stay in Venice was altogether incompatible with the exhausted state of his finances, and that, if he extended his sojourn here beyond the appointed time, he could not reckon on receiving funds from his court. On this occasion, I learned what had hitherto been a secret to me, namely, that the prince had, without the knowledge of his other brothers, received from his sister, the reigning ----- of --------, considerable loans, which she would gladly double if his court left him in the lurch. This sister, who, as you know, is a pious enthusiast, thinks that the large savings which she makes at a very economical court cannot be deposited in better hands than in those of a brother whose wise benevolence she well knows, and whose character she warmly honors. I have, indeed, known for some time that a very close intercourse has been kept up between the two, and that many letters have been exchanged; but, as the prince's own resources have hitherto always been sufficient to cover his expenditure, I had never guessed at this hidden channel. It is clear, therefore, that the prince must have had some expenses which have been and still are unknown to me; but if I can judge of them by his general character, they will certainly not be of such a description as to tend to his disgrace. And yet I thought I understood him thoroughly. After this disclosure, I of course did not hesitate to make known to him the marquis' offer, which, to my no small surprise, he immediately accepted. He gave me the authority to transact the business with the marquis in whatever way I thought most advisable, and then immediately to settle the account with the usurer. To his sister he proposed to write without delay.

It was morning when we separated. However disagreeable this affair is to me for more than one reason, the worst of it is that it seems to threaten a longer residence in Venice. From the prince's passion I rather augur good than evil. It is, perhaps, the most powerful method of withdrawing him from his metaphysical dreams to the concerns and feelings of real life. It will have its crisis, and, like an illness produced by artificial means, will eradicate the natural disorder.

Farewell, my dear friend. I have written down these incidents immediately upon their occurrence. The post starts immediately; you will receive this letter on the same day as my last.

LETTER VI.

BARON F------ TO COUNT O-------. June 20.

This Civitella is certainly one of the most obliging personages in the world. The prince had scarcely left me the other day before I received a note from the marquis enforcing his former offers with renewed earnestness. I instantly forwarded, in the prince's name, a bond for six thousand zechins; in less than half an hour it was returned, with double the sum required, in notes and gold. The prince at length assented to this increase, but insisted that the bond, which was drawn only for six weeks, should be accepted.

The whole of the present week has been consumed in inquiries after the mysterious Greek. Biondello set all his engines to work, but until now in vain. He certainly discovered the gondolier; but from him he could learn nothing, save that the ladies had disembarked on the island of Murano, where they entered two sedan chairs which were waiting for them. He supposed them to be English because they spoke a foreign language, and had paid him in gold. He did not even know their guide, but believed him to be a glass manufacturer from Murano. We were now, at least, certain that we must not look for her in the Giudecca, and that in all probability she lived in the island of Murano; but, unluckily, the description the prince gave of her was not such as to make her recognizable by a third party. The passionate interest with which he had regarded her had hindered him from observing her minutely; for all the minor details, which other people would not have failed to notice, had escaped his observation; from his description one would have sooner expected to find her prototype in the works of Ariosto or Tasso than on a Venetian island. Besides, our inquiries had to be conducted with the utmost caution, in order not to become prejudicial to the lady, or to excite undue attention. As Biondello was the only man besides the prince who had seen her, even through her veil, and could therefore recognize her, he strove to be as much as possible in all the places where she was likely to appear; the life of the poor man, during the whole week, was a continual race through all the streets of Venice. In the Greek church, particularly, every inquiry was made, but always with the same ill-success; and the prince, whose impatience increased with every successive failure, was at last obliged to wait till Saturday, with what patience he might. His restlessness was excessive. Nothing interested him, nothing could fix his attention. He was in constant feverish excitement; he fled from society, but the evil increased in solitude. He had never been so much besieged by visitors as in this week. His approaching departure had been announced, and everybody crowded to see him. It was necessary to occupy the attention of the people in order to lull their suspicions, and to amuse the prince with the view of diverting his mind from its all-engrossing object. In this emergency Civitella hit upon play; and, for the purpose of driving away most of the visitors, proposed that the stakes should be high. He hoped by awakening in the prince a transient liking for play, from which it would afterwards be easy to wean him, to destroy the romantic bent of his passion. "The cards," said Civitella, "have saved me from many a folly which I had intended to commit, and repaired many which I had already perpetrated. At the faro table I have often recovered my tranquillity of mind, of which a pair of bright eyes had robbed me, and women never had more power over me than when I had not money enough to play."

I will not enter into a discussion as to how far Civitella was right; but the remedy we had hit upon soon began to be worse than the disease it was intended to cure. The prince, who could only make the game at all interesting to himself by staking extremely high, soon overstepped all bounds. He was quite out of his element. Everything he did seemed to be done in a passion; all his actions betrayed the uneasiness of his mind. You know his general indifference to money; he seemed now to have become totally insensible to its value. Gold flowed through his hands like water. As he played without the slightest caution he lost almost invariably. He lost immense sums, for he staked like a desperate gamester. Dearest O------- , with an aching heart I write it, in four days he had lost above twelve thousand zechins.

Do not reproach me. I blame myself sufficiently. But how could I prevent it? Could I do more than warn him? I did all that was in my power, and cannot find myself guilty. Civitella, too, lost not a little; I won about six hundred zechins. The unprecedented ill-luck of the prince excited general attention, and therefore he would not leave off playing. Civitella, who is always ready to oblige him, immediately advanced him the required sum. The deficit is made up; but the prince owes the marquis twenty-four thousand zechins. Oh, how I long for the savings of his pious sister. Are all sovereigns so, my dear friend? The prince behaves as though he had done the marquis a great honor, and he, at any rate, plays his part well.

Civitella sought to quiet me by saying that this recklessness, this extraordinary ill-luck, would be most effectual in bringing the prince to his senses. The money, he said, was of no consequence. He himself would not feel the loss in the least, and would be happy to serve the prince, at any moment, with three times the amount. The cardinal also assured me that his nephew's intentions were honest, and that he should be ready to assist him in carrying them out.

The most unfortunate thing was that these tremendous sacrifices did not even effect their object. One would have thought that the prince would at least feel some interest in his play. But such was not the case. His thoughts were wandering far away, and the passion which we wished to stifle by his ill-luck in play seemed, on the contrary, only to gather strength. When, for instance, a decisive stroke was about to be played, and every one's eyes were fixed, full of expectation, on the board, his were searching for Biondello, in order to catch the news he might have brought him, from the expression of his countenance. Biondello brought no tidings, and his master's losses continued.

The gains, however, fell into very needy hands. A few "your excellencies," whom scandal reports to be in the habit of carrying home their frugal dinner from the market in their senatorial caps, entered our house as beggars, and left it with well-lined purses. Civitella pointed them out to me. "Look," said he, "how many poor devils make their fortunes by one great man taking a whim into his head. This is what I like to see. It is princely and royal. A great man must, even by his failings, make some one happy, like a river which by its overflowing fertilizes the neighboring fields."

Civitella has a noble and generous way of thinking, but the prince owes him twenty-four thousand zechins.

At length the long-wished-for Saturday arrived, and my master insisted upon going, directly after dinner, to the church. He stationed himself in the chapel where he had first seen the unknown, but in such a way as not to be immediately observed. Biondello had orders to keep watch at the church door, and to enter into conversation with the attendant of the ladies. I had taken upon myself to enter, like a chance passenger, into the same gondola with them on their return, in order to follow their track if the other schemes should fail. At the spot where the gondolier said he had landed them the last time two sedans were stationed; the chamberlain, Z------, was ordered to follow in a separate gondola, in order to trace the retreat of the unknown, if all else should fail. The prince wished to give himself wholly up to the pleasure of seeing her, and, if possible, try to make her acquaintance in the church. Civitella was to keep out of the way altogether, as his reputation among the women of Venice was so bad that his presence could not have failed to excite the suspicions of the lady. You see, dear count, it was not through any want of precaution on our part that the fair unknown escaped us.

Never, perhaps, was there offered up in any church such ardent prayers for success, and never were hopes so cruelly disappointed. The prince waited till after sunset, starting in expectation at every sound which approached the chapel, and at every creaking of the church door. Seven full hours passed, and no Greek lady. I need not describe his state of mind. You know what hope deferred is, hope which one has nourished unceasingly for seven days and nights.

LETTER VII.

BARON VON F------ TO COUNT VON O------- July.

The mysterious unknown of the prince reminded Marquis Civitella of a romantic incident which happened to himself a short time since, and, to divert the prince, he offered to relate it. I will give it you in his own words; but the lively spirit which he infuses into all he tells will be lost in my narration.

(Here follows the subjoined fragment, which appeared in the eighth part of the Thalia, and was originally intended for the second volume of the Ghost-Seer. It found a place here after Schiller had given up the idea of completing the Ghost-Seer.)

"In the spring of last year," began Civitella, "I had the misfortune to embroil myself with the Spanish ambassador, a gentleman who, in his seventieth year, had been guilty of the folly of wishing to marry a Roman girl of eighteen. His vengeance pursued me, and my friends advised me to secure my safety by a timely flight, and to keep out of the way until the hand of nature, or an adjustment of differences, had secured me from the wrath of this formidable enemy. As I felt it too severe a punishment to quit Venice altogether, I took up my abode in a distant quarter of the town, where I lived in a lonely house, under a feigned name, keeping myself concealed by day, and devoting the night to the society of my friends and of pleasure.

"My windows looked upon a garden, the west side of which was bounded by the walls of a convent, while towards the east it jutted out into the Laguna in the form of a little peninsula. The garden was charmingly situated, but little frequented. It was my custom every morning, after my friends had left me, to spend a few moments at the window before retiring to rest, to see the sun rise over the Adriatic, and then to bid him goodnight. If you, my dear prince, have not yet enjoyed this pleasure, I recommend exactly this station, the only eligible one perhaps in all Venice to enjoy so splendid a prospect in perfection. A purple twilight hangs over the deep, and a golden mist on the Laguna announces the sun's approach. The heavens and the sea are wrapped in expectant silence. In two seconds the orb of day appears, casting a flood of fiery light on the waves. It is an enchanting sight.

"One morning, when I was, according to custom, enjoying the beauty of this prospect, I suddenly discovered that I was not the only spectator of the scene. I fancied I heard voices in the garden, and turning to the quarter whence the sound proceeded, I perceived a gondola steering for the land. In a few moments I saw figures walking at a slow pace up the avenue. They were a man and a woman, accompanied by a little negro. The female was clothed in white, and had a brilliant on her finger. It was not light enough to perceive more.

"My curiosity was raised. Doubtless a rendezvous of a pair of lovers-- but in such a place, and at so unusual an hour! It was scarcely three o'clock, and everything was still veiled in dusky twilight. The incident seemed to me novel and proper for a romance, and I waited to see the end.

"I soon lost sight of them among the foliage of the garden, and some time elapsed before they again emerged to view. Meanwhile a delightful song was heard. It proceeded from the gondolier, who was in this manner shortening the time, and was answered by a comrade a short way off. They sang stanzas from Tasso; time and place were in unison, and the melody sounded sweetly, in the profound silence around.

"Day in the meantime had dawned, and objects were discerned more plainly. I sought my people, whom I found walking hand-in-hand up a broad walk, often standing still, but always with their backs turned towards me, and proceeding further from my residence. Their noble, easy carriage convinced me at once that they were people of rank, and the splendid figure of the lady made me augur as much of her beauty. They appeared to converse but little; the lady, however, more than her companion. In the spectacle of the rising sun, which now burst out in all its splendor, they seemed to take not the slightest interest.

"While I was employed in adjusting my glass, in order to bring them into view as closely as possible, they suddenly disappeared down a side path, and some time elapsed before I regained sight of them. The sun had now fully risen; they were approaching straight towards me, with their eyes fixed upon where I stood. What a heavenly form did I behold! Was it illusion, or the magic effect of the beautiful light? I thought I beheld a supernatural being, for my eyes quailed before the angelic brightness of her look. So much loveliness combined with so much dignity!--so much mind, and so much blooming youth! It is in vain I attempt to describe it. I had never seen true beauty till that moment.

"In the heat of conversation they lingered near me, and I had full opportunity to contemplate her. Scarcely, however, had I cast my eyes upon her companion, but even her beauty was not powerful enough to fix my attention. He appeared to be a man still in the prime of life, rather slight, and of a tall, noble figure. Never have I beheld so much mind, so much noble expression, in a human countenance. Though perfectly secured from observation, I was unable to meet the lightning glance that shot from beneath his dark eyebrows. There was a moving expression of sorrow about his eyes, but an expression of benevolence about the mouth which relieved the settled gravity spread over his whole countenance. A certain cast of features, not quite European, together with his dress, which appeared to have been chosen with inimitable good taste from the most varied costumes, gave him a peculiar air, which not a little heightened the impression produced by his appearance. A degree of wildness in his looks warranted the supposition that he was an enthusiast, but his deportment and carriage showed that his character had been formed by mixing in society."

Z--------, who you know must always give utterance to what he thinks, could contain himself no longer. "Our Armenian!" cried he. "Our very Armenian, and nobody else."

"What Armenian, if one may ask?" inquired Civitella.

"Has no one told you of the farce?" replied the prince. "But no interruption! I begin to feel interested in your hero. Pray continue your narrative."

"There was something inexplicable in his whole demeanor," continued Civitella. "His eyes were fixed upon his companion with an expression of anxiety and passion, but the moment they met hers he looked down abashed. 'Is the man beside himself!' thought I. I could stand for ages and gaze at nothing else but her.

"The foliage again concealed them from my sight. Long, long did I look for their reappearance, but in vain. At length I caught sight of them from another window.

"They were standing before the basin of a fountain at some distance apart, and both wrapped in deep silence. They had, probably, remained some time in the same position. Her clear and intelligent eyes were resting inquiringly on his, and seemed as if they would imbibe every thought from him as it revealed itself in his countenance. He, as if he wanted courage to look directly into her face, furtively sought its reflection in the watery mirror before him, or gazed steadfastly at the dolphin which bore the water to the basin. Who knows how long this silent scene might have continued could the lady have endured it? With the most bewitching grace the lovely girl advanced towards him, and passing her arm round his neck, raised his hand to her lips. Calmly and unmoved the strange being suffered her caresses, but did not return them.

"This scene moved me strangely. It was the man that chiefly excited my sympathy and interest. Some violent emotion seemed to struggle in his breast; it was as if some irresistible force drew him towards her, while an unseen arm held him back. Silent, but agonizing, was the struggle, and beautiful the temptation. 'No,' I thought, 'he attempts too much; he will, he must yield.'

"At his silent intimation the young negro disappeared. I now expected some touching scene--a prayer on bended knees, and a reconciliation sealed with glowing kisses. But no! nothing of the kind occurred. The incomprehensible being took from his pocketbook a sealed packet, and placed it in the hands of the lady. Sadness overcast her face as she she looked at it, and a tear bedewed her eye.

"After a short silence they separated. At this moment an elderly lady advanced from one of the sidewalks, who had remained at a distance, and whom I now first discovered. She and the fair girl slowly advanced along the path, and, while they were earnestly engaged in conversation, the stranger took the opportunity of remaining behind. With his eyes turned towards her, he stood irresolute, at one instant making a rapid step forward, and in the next retreating. In another moment he had disappeared in the copse.

"The women at length look round, seem uneasy at not finding him, and pause as if to await his coming. He comes not. Anxious glances are cast around, and steps are redoubled. My eyes aid in searching through the garden; he comes not, he is nowhere to be seen.

"Suddenly I see a plash in the canal, and see a gondola moving from the shore. It is he, and I scarcely can refrain from calling to him. Now the whole thing is clear--it was a parting.

"She appears to have a presentiment of what has happened. With a speed that her companion cannot use she hastens to the shore. Too late! Quick as the arrow in its flight the gondola bounds forward, and soon nothing is visible but a white handkerchief fluttering in the air from afar. Soon after this I saw the fair incognita and her companion cross the water.

"When I awoke from a short sleep I could not help smiling at my delusion. My fancy had incorporated these events in my dreams until truth itself seemed a dream. A maiden, fair as an houri, wandering beneath my windows at break of day with her lover--and a lover who did not know how to make a better use of such an hour. Surely these supplied materials for the composition of a picture which might well occupy the fancy of a dreamer! But the dream had been too lovely for me not to desire its renewal again and again; nay, even the garden had become more charming in my sight since my imagination had peopled it with such attractive forms. Several cheerless days that succeeded this eventful morning drove me from the window, but the first fine evening involuntarily drew me back to my post of observation. Judge of my surprise when after a short search I caught sight of the white dress of my incognita! Yes, it was she herself. I had not dreamed!

"Her former companion was with her, and led by the hand a little boy; but the fair girl herself walked apart, and seemed absorbed in thought. All spots were visited that had been rendered memorable by the presence of her friend. She paused for a long time before the basin, and her fixed gaze seemed to seek on its crystal mirror the reflection of one beloved form.

"Although her noble beauty had attracted me when I first saw her the impression produced was even stronger on this occasion, although perhaps at the same time more conducive to gentler emotions. I had now ample opportunity of considering this divine form; the surprise of the first impression gradually gave place to softer feelings. The glory that seemed to invest her had departed, and I saw before me the loveliest of women, and felt my senses inflamed. In a moment the resolution was formed that she must be mine.

"While I was deliberating whether I should descend and approach her, or whether before I ventured on such a step it would not be better to obtain information regarding her, a door opened in the convent wall, through which there advanced a Carmelite monk. The sound of his approach roused the lady, and I saw her advance with hurried steps towards him. He drew from his bosom a paper, which she eagerly grasped, while a vivid color instantaneously suffused her countenance.

"At this moment I was called from the window by the arrival of my usual evening visitor. I carefully avoided approaching the spot again as I had no desire to share my conquest with another. For a whole hour I was obliged to endure this painful constraint before I could succeed in freeing myself from my importunate guest, and when I hastened to the window all had disappeared.

"The garden was empty when I entered it; no vessel of any kind was visible in the canal; no trace of people on any side; I neither knew whence she had come nor whither she had gone. While I was looking round me in all directions I observed something white upon the ground. On drawing near I found it was a piece of paper folded in the shape of a note. What could it be but the letter which the Carmelite had brought? 'Happy discovery!' I exclaimed; 'this will reveal the whole secret, and make me master of her fate.'

"The letter was sealed with a sphinx, had no superscription, and was written in cyphers; this, however, did not discourage me, for I have some knowledge of this mode of writing. I copied it hastily, as there was every reason to expect that she would soon miss it and return in search of it. If she should not find it she would regard its loss as an evidence that the garden was resorted to by different persons, and such a discovery might easily deter her from visiting it again. And what worse fortune could attend my hopes.

"That which I had conjectured actually took place, and I had scarcely ended my copy when she reappeared with her former companion, anxiously intent on the search. I attached the note to a tile which I had detached from the roof, and dropped it at a spot which she would pass. Her gracefully expressed joy at finding it rewarded me for my generosity. She examined it in every part with keen, searching glances, as if she were seeking to detect the unhallowed hands that might have touched it; but the contented look with which she hid it in her bosom showed that she was free from all suspicion. She went, and the parting glance she threw on the garden seemed expressive of gratitude to the guardian deities of the spot, who had so faithfully watched over the secret of her heart.

"I now hastened to decipher the letter. After trying several languages, I at length succeeded by the use of English. Its contents were so remarkable that my memory still retains a perfect recollection of them."

I am interrupted, and must give you the conclusion on a future occasion.

LETTER VIII.

BARON F------ TO COUNT O------- August.

In truth, my dearest friend, you do the good Biondello injustice. The suspicion you entertain against him is unfounded, and while I allow you full liberty to condemn all Italians generally, I must maintain that this one at least is an honest man.

You think it singular that a person of such brilliant endowments and such exemplary conduct should debase himself to enter the service of another if he were not actuated by secret motives; and these, you further conclude, must necessarily be of a suspicious character. But where is the novelty of a man of talent and of merit endeavoring to win favor with a prince who has the power of establishing his fortune? Is there anything derogatory in serving the prince? and has not Biondello clearly shown that his devotion is purely personal by confessing that he earnestly desired to make a certain request of the prince? The whole mystery will, therefore, no doubt be revealed when he acquaints him of his wishes. He may certainly be actuated by secret motives, but why may these not be innocent in their nature?

You think it strange that this Biondello should have kept all his great talents concealed, and in no way have attracted attention during the early months of our acquaintance with him, when you were still with us. This I grant; but what opportunity had he then of distinguishing himself? The prince had not yet called his powers into requisition, and chance, therefore, could alone aid us in discovering his talents.

He very recently gave a proof of his devotion and honesty of purpose which must at once annihilate all your doubts. The prince was watched; measures were being taken to gain information regarding his mode of life, associates, and general habits. I know not with whom this inquisitiveness originated.

Let me beg your attention, however, to what I am about to relate:--

There is a house in St. George's which Biondello is in the habit of frequenting. He probably finds some peculiar attractions there, but of this I know nothing. It happened a few days ago that he there met assembled together a party of civil and military officers in the service of the government, old acquaintances and jovial comrades of his own. Surprise and pleasure were expressed on all sides at this meeting. Their former good-fellowship was re-established; and after each in turn had related his own history up to the present time, Biondello was called upon to give an account of his life; this he did in a few words. He was congratulated on his new position; his companions had heard accounts of the splendid footing on which the Prince of -------'s establishment was maintained; of his liberality, especially to persons who showed discretion in keeping secrets; the prince's connection with the Cardinal A------i was well known, he was said to be addicted to play, etc. Biondello's surprise at this is observed, and jokes are passed upon the mystery which he tries to keep up, although it is well known that he is the emissary of the Prince of ------. The two lawyers of the party make him sit down between them; their glasses are repeatedly emptied, he is urged to drink, but excuses himself on the grounds of inability to bear wine; at last, however, he yields to their wishes, in order that he may the better pretend intoxication.

"Yes!" cried one of the lawyers, "Biondello understands his business, but he has not yet learned all the tricks of the trade; he is but a novice."

"What have I still to learn?" ask Biondello.

"You understand the art of keeping a secret," remarked the other; "but you have still to learn that of parting with it to advantage."

"Am I likely to find a purchaser for any that I may have to dispose of?" asked Biondello.

On this the other guests withdrew from the apartment, and left him alone with his two neighbors, who continued the conversation in the same strain. The substance of the whole was, however, briefly as follows: Biondello was to procure them certain information regarding the intercourse of the prince with the cardinal and his nephew, acquaint them with the source from whence the prince derived his money, and to intercept all letters written to Count O------. Biondello put them off to a future occasion, but he was unsuccessful in his attempts to draw from them the name of the person by whom they were employed. From the splendid nature of the proposals made to him it was evident, however, that they emanated from some influential and extremely wealthy party.

Last night he related the whole occurrence to the prince, whose first impulse was without further ceremony to secure the maneuverers at once, but to this Biondello strongly objected. He urged that he would be obliged to set them at liberty again, and that, in this case, he should endanger not only his credit among this class of men, but even his life. All these men were connected together, and bound by one common interest, each one making the cause of the others his own; in fact, he would rather make enemies of the senate of Venice than be regarded by these men as a traitor--and, besides, he could no longer be useful to the prince if he lost the confidence of this class of people.

We have pondered and conjectured much as to the source of all this. Who is there in Venice that can care to know what money my master receives or pays out, what passess between Cardinal A-----i and himself, and what I write to you? Can it be some scheme of the Prince of ---d-----, or is the Armenian again on the alert?

LETTER IX.

BARON F------ TO COUNT O-------. August.

The prince is revelling in love and bliss. He has recovered his fair Greek. I must relate to you how this happened.

A traveller, who had crossed from Chiozza, gave the prince so animated an account of the beauty of this place, which is charmingly situated on the shores of the gulf, that he became very anxious to see it. Yesterday was fixed upon for the excursion; and, in order to avoid all restraint and display, no one was to accompany him but Z------- and myself, together with Biondello, as my master wished to remain unknown. We found a vessel ready to start, and engaged our passage at once. The company was very mixed but not numerous, and the passage was made without the occurrence of any circumstance worthy of notice.

Chiozza is built, like Venice, on a foundation of wooden piles, and is said to contain about forty thousand inhabitants. There are but few of the higher classes resident there, but one meets sailors and fishermen at every step.

Whoever appears in a peruke, or a cloak, is regarded as an aristocrat--a rich man; the cap and overcoat are here the insignia of the poor. The situation is certainly very lovely, but it will not bear a comparison with Venice.

We did not remain long, for the captain, who had more passengers for the return voyage, was obliged to be in Venice at an early hour, and there was nothing at Chiozza to make the prince desirous of remaining. All the passengers were on board when we reached the vessel. As we had found it so difficult to place ourselves on a social footing with the company on the outward passage, we determined on this occasion to secure a cabin to ourselves. The prince inquired who the new-comers were, and was informed that they were a Dominican and some ladies, who were returning to Venice. My master evincing no curiosity to see them, we immediately betook ourselves to our cabin.

The Greek was the subject of our conversation throughout the whole passage, as she had been during our former transit. The prince dwelt with ardor on her appearance in the church; and whilst numerous plans were in turn devised and rejected, hours passed like a moment of time, and we were already in sight of Venice. Some of the passengers now disembarked, the Dominican amongst the number. The captain went to the ladies, who, as we now first learned, had been separated from us by only a thin wooden partition, and asked them where they wished to land. The island of Murano was named in reply to his inquiry, and the house indicated. "The island of Murano!" exclaimed the prince, who seemed suddenly struck by a startling presentiment. Before I could reply to his exclamation, Biondello rushed into the cabin. "Do you know," asked he eagerly, "who is on board with us?" The prince started to his feet, as Biondello continued, "She is here! she herself! I have just spoken to her companion!"

The prince hurried out. He felt as if he could not breathe in our narrow cabin, and I believe at that moment as if the whole world would have been too narrow for him. A thousand conflicting feelings struggled for the mastery in his heart; his knees trembled, and his countenance was alternately flushed and pallid. I sympathized and participated in his emotion, but I cannot by words convey to your mind any idea of the state in which he was.

When we stopped at Murano, the prince sprang on shore. She advanced from her cabin. I read in the face of the prince that it was indeed the Greek. One glance was sufficient to dispel all doubt on that point. A more lovely creature I have never seen. Even the prince's glowing descriptions fell far short of the reality. A radiant blush suffused her face when she saw my master. She must have heard all we said, and could not fail to know that she herself had been the subject of our conversation. She exchanged a significant glance with her companion, which seemed to say, "That is he;" and then cast her eyes to the ground with diffident confusion. On placing her foot on the narrow plank, which had been thrown from the vessel to the shore, she seemed anxiously to hesitate, less, as it seemed to me, from the fear of falling than from her inability to cross the board without assistance, which was proffered her by the outstretched arm of the prince. Necessity overcame her reluctance, and, accepting the aid of his hand, she stepped on shore. Excessive mental agitation had rendered the prince uncourteous, and he wholly forgot to offer his services to the other lady--but what was there that he would not have forgotten at this moment? My attention in atoning for the remissness of the prince prevented my hearing the commencement of a conversation which had begun between him and the young Greek, while I had been helping the other lady on shore.

He was still holding her hand in his, probably from absence of mind, and without being conscious of the fact.

"This is not the first time, Signora, that--that"--he stopped short, unable to finish the sentence.

"I think I remember" she faltered.

"We met in the church of ---------," said he, quickly.

"Yes, it was in the church of ---------," she rejoined.

"And could I have supposed that this day would have brought me--"

Here she gently withdrew her hand from his--he was evidently embarrassed; but Biondello, who had in the meantime been speaking to the servant, now came to his aid.

"Si-nor," said he, "the ladies had ordered sedans to be in readiness for them; they have not yet come, for we are here before the expected time. But there is a garden close by in which you may remain until the crowd has dispersed."

The proposal was accepted; you may conceive with what alacrity on the part of the prince! We remained in the garden till late in the evening; and, fortunately, Z-------- and myself so effectually succeeded in occupying the attention of the elder lady that the prince was enabled, undisturbed, to carry on his conversation with the fair Greek. You will easily believe that he made good use of his time, when I tell you that he obtained permission to visit her. At the very moment that I am now writing he is with her; on his return I shall be able to give you further particulars regarding her.

When we got home yesterday we found that the long-expected remittances had arrived from our court; but at the same time the prince received a letter which excited his indignation to the highest pitch. He has been recalled, and that in a tone and manner to which he is wholly unaccustomed. He immediately wrote a reply in a similar spirit, and intends remaining. The remittances are only just sufficient to pay the interest on the capital which he owes. We are looking with impatience for a reply from his sister.

LETTER X.

BARON F------ TO COUNT O------- September.

The prince has fallen out with his court, and all resources have consequently been cut off from home.

The term of six weeks, at the end of which my master was to pay the marquis, has already elapsed several days; but still no remittances have been forwarded, either from his cousin, of whom he had earnestly requested an additional allowance in advance, or from his sister. You may readily suppose that Civitella has not reminded him of his debt; the prince's memory is, however, all the more faithful. Yesterday morning at length brought an answer from the seat of government.

We had shortly before concluded a new arrangement with the master of our hotel, and the prince had publicly announced his intention to remain here sometime longer. Without uttering a word my master put the letter into my hand. His eyes sparkled, and I could read the contents in his face.

Can you believe it, dear O; all my master's proceedings here are known at and have been most calumniously misrepresented by an abominable tissue of lies? "Information has been received," says the letter, amongst other things, "to the effect that the prince has for some time past belied his former character, and adopted a node of conduct totally at variance with his former exemplary manner of acting and thinking." "It is known," the writer says, "that he has addicted himself with the greatest excess to women and play; that he is overwhelmed with debts; puts his confidence in visionaries and charlatans, who pretend to have power over spirits; maintains suspicious relations with Roman Catholic prelates, and keeps up a degree of state which exceeds both his rank and his means. Nay, it is even said, that he is about to bring this highly offensive conduct to a climax by apostacy to the Church of Rome! and in order to clear himself from this last charge he is required to return immediately. A banker at Venice, to whom he must make known the true amount of his debts, has received instructions to satisfy his creditors immediately after his departure; for, under existing circumstances, it does not appear expedient to remit the money directly into his hands."

What accusations, and what a mode of preferring them. I read the letter again and again, in the hope of discovering some expression that admitted of a milder construction, but in vain; it was wholly incomprehensible.

Z------- now reminded me of the secret inquiries which had been made some time before of Biondello. The true nature of the inquiries and circumstances all coincided. He had falsely ascribed them to the Armenian; but now the source from whence the came was very evident. Apostacy! But who can have any interest in calumniating my master so scandalously? I should fear it was some machination of the Prince of ---d-----, who is determined on driving him from Venice.

In the meantime the prince remained absorbed in thought, with his eyes fixed on the ground. His continued silence alarmed me. I threw myself at his feet. "For God's sake, your highness," I cried, "moderate your feelings--you will--nay, you shall have satisfaction. Leave the whole affair to me. Let me be your emissary. It is beneath your dignity to reply to such accusations; but you will not, I know, refuse me the privilege of doing so for you. The name of your calumniator must be given up, and -------'s eyes must be opened."

At this moment we were interrupted by the entrance of Civitella, who inquired with surprise into the cause of our agitation. Z------- and I did not answer; but the prince, who had long ceased to make any distinction between him and us, and who, besides, was too much excited to listen to the dictates of prudence, desired me to communicate the contents of the letter to him. On my hesitating to obey him, he snatched the letter from my hand and gave it to the marquis.

"I am in your debt, marquis," said he, as Civitella gave him back the letter, after perusing it, with evident astonishment, "but do not let that circumstance occasion you any uneasiness; grant me but a respite of twenty days, and you shall be fully satisfied."

"Do I deserve this at your hands, gracious prince?" exclaimed Civitella, with extreme emotion.

"You have refrained from pressing me, and I gratefully appreciate your delicacy. In twenty days, as I before said, you shall be fully satisfied."

"But how is this?" asked Civitella, with agitation and surprise. "What means all this? I cannot comprehend it."

We explained to him all that we knew, and his indignation was unbounded. The prince, he asserted, must insist upon full satisfaction; the insult was unparalleled.

In the meanwhile he implored him to make unlimited use of his fortune and his credit.

When the marquis left us the prince still continued silent. He paced the apartment with quick and determined steps, as if some strange and unusual emotion were agitating his frame. At length he paused, muttering between his teeth, "Congratulate yourself; he died at ten o'clock."

We looked at him in terror.

"Congratulate yourself," he repeated. "Did he not say that I should congratulate myself? What could he have meant?"

"What has reminded you of those words?" I asked; "and what have they to do with the present business?"

"I did not then understand what the man meant, but now I do. Oh, it is intolerable to be subject to a master."

"Gracious prince!"

"Who can make us feel our dependence. Ha! it must be sweet, indeed."

He again paused. His looks alarmed me, for I had never before seen him thus agitated.

"Whether a man be poorest of the poor," he continued, "or the next heir to the throne, it is all one and the same thing. There is but one difference between men--to obey or to command."

He again glanced over the letter.

"You know the man," he continued, "who has dared to write these words to me. Would you salute him in the street if fate had not made him your master? By Heaven, there is something great in a crown."

He went on in this strain, giving expression to many things which I dare not trust to paper. On this occasion the prince confided a circumstance to me which alike surprised and terrified me, and which may be followed by the most alarming consequences. We have hitherto been entirely deceived regarding the family relations of the court of --------.

He answered the letter on the spot, notwithstanding my earnest entreaty that he should postpone doing so; and the strain in which he wrote leaves no ground to hope for a favorable settlement of those differences.

You are no doubt impatient, dear O------, to hear something definite with respect to the Greek; but in truth I have very little to tell you. From the prince I can learn nothing, as he has been admitted into her confidence, and is, I believe, bound to secrecy. The fact has, however, transpired that she is not a Greek, as we supposed, but a German of the highest descent. From a certain report that has reached me, it would appear that her mother is of the most exalted rank, and that she is the fruit of an unfortunate amour which was once talked of all over Europe. A course of secret persecution to which she had been exposed, in consequence of her origin, compelled her to seek protection in Venice, and to adopt that concealment which had rendered it impossible for the prince to discover her retreat. The respect with which the prince speaks of her, and a certain deferential deportment which he maintains towards her, appear to corroborate the truth of this report.

He is devoted to her with a fearful intensity of passion which increases day by day. In the earliest stage of their acquaintance but few interviews were granted; but after the first week the separations were of shorter duration, and now there is scarce a day on which the prince is not with her. Whole evenings pass without our even seeing him, and when he is not with her she appears to form the sole object of his thoughts. His whole being seems metamorphosed. He goes about as if wrapped in a dream, and nothing that formerly interested him has now power to arrest his attention even for a moment.

How will this end, my dear friend? I tremble for the future. The rupture with his court has placed my master in a state of humiliating dependence on one sole person--the Marquis Civitella. This man is now master of our secrets--of our whole fate. Will he always conduct himself as nobly as he does now? Are his good intentions to be relied upon; and is it expedient to confide so much weight and power to one person--even were he the best of men? The prince's sister has again been written to--the result of this fresh appeal you shall learn in my next letter.

COUNT O------- IN CONTINUATION.

This letter never reached me. Three months passed without my receiving any tidings from Venice,--an interruption to our correspondence which the sequel but too clearly explained. All my friend's letters to me had been kept back and suppressed. My emotion may be conceived when, in the December of the same year, the following letter reached me by mere accident (as it afterwards appeared), owing to the sudden illness of Biondello, into whose hands it had been committed.

"You do not write; you do not answer me. Come, I entreat you, come on the wings of friendship! Our hopes are fled! Read the enclosed,--all our hopes are at an end!

"The wounds of the marquis are reported mortal. The cardinal vows vengeance, and his bravos are in pursuit of the prince. My master--oh! my unhappy master! Has it come to this! Wretched, horrible fate! We are compelled to hide ourselves, like malefactors, from assassins and creditors.

"I am writing to you from the convent of --------, where the prince has found an asylum. At this moment he is resting on his hard couch by my side, and is sleeping--but, alas! it is only the sleep of deadly exhaustion, that will but give him new strength for new trials. During the ten days that she was ill no sleep closed his eyes. I was present when the body was opened. Traces of poison were detected. To-day she is to be buried.

"Alas! dearest O------, my heart is rent. I have lived through scenes that can never be effaced from my memory. I stood beside her deathbed. She departed like a saint, and her last strength was spent in trying with persuasive eloquence to lead her lover into the path that she was treading in her way to heaven. Our firmness was completely gone--the prince alone maintained his fortitude, and although he suffered a triple agony of death with her, he yet retained strength of mind sufficient to refuse the last prayer of the pious enthusiast."

This letter contained the following enclosure:

TO THE PRINCE OF --------, FROM HIS SISTER.

"The one sole redeeming church which has made so glorious a conquest of the Prince of -------- will surely not refuse to supply him with means to pursue the mode of life to which she owes this conquest. I have tears and prayers for one that has gone astray, but nothing further to bestow on one so worthless! HENRIETTE."

I instantly threw myself into a carriage--travelled night and day, and in the third week I was in Venice. My speed availed nothing. I had come to bring comfort and help to an unhappy one, but I found a happy one who needed not my weak aid. F------- was ill when I arrived, and unable to see me, but the following note was brought to me from him.

"Return, dearest O-----, to whence you came. The prince no longer needs you or me. His debts have been paid; the cardinal is reconciled to him, and the marquis has recovered. Do you remember the Armenian who perplexed us so much last year? In his arms you will find the prince, who five days since attended mass for the first time."

Notwithstanding all this I earnestly sought an interview with the prince, but was refused. By the bedside of my friend I learnt the particulars of this strange story.

THE SPORT OF DESTINY

ALOYSIUS VON G------ was the son of a citizen of distinction, in the service of -------, and the germs of his fertile genius had been early developed by a liberal education. While yet very young, but already well grounded in the principles of knowledge, he entered the military service of his sovereign, to whom he soon made himself known as a young man of great merit and still greater promise. G------ was now in the full glow of youth, so also was the prince. G------ was ardent and enterprising; the prince, of a similar disposition, loved such characters. Endued with brilliant wit and a rich fund of information, G------ possessed the art of ingratiating himself with all around him; he enlivened every circle in which he moved by his felicitous humor, and infused life and spirit into every subject that came before him. The prince had discernment enough to appreciate in another those virtues which he himself possessed in an eminent degree.

Everything which G------ undertook, even to his very sports, had an air of grandeur; no difficulties could daunt him, no failures vanquish his perseverance. The value of these qualities was increased by an attractive person, the perfect image of blooming health and herculean strength, and heightened by the eloquent expression natural to an active mind; to these was added a certain native and unaffected dignity, chastened and subdued by a noble modesty. If the prince was charmed with the intellectual attractions of his young companion, his fascinating exterior irresistibly captivated his senses. Similarity of age, of tastes, and of character soon produced an intimacy between them, which possessed all the strength of friendship and all the warmth and fervor of the most passionate love.

G------ rose with rapidity from one promotion to another; but whatever the extent of favors conferred they still seemed in the estimation of the prince to fall short of his deserts. His fortune advanced with gigantic strides, for the author of his greatness was his devoted admirer and his warmest friend. Not yet twenty-two years of age, he already saw himself placed on an eminence hitherto attained only by the most fortunate at the close of their career. But his active spirit was incapable of reposing long in the lap of indolent vanity, or of contenting itself with the glittering pomp of an elevated office, to perform the behests of which he was conscious of possessing both the requisite courage and the abilities. Whilst the prince was engaged in rounds of pleasure, his young favorite buried himself among archives and books, and devoted himself with laborious assiduity to affairs of state, in which he at length became so expert that every matter of importance passed through his hands. From the companion of his pleasures he soon became first councillor and minister, and finally the ruler of his sovereign. In a short time there was no road to the prince's favor but through him. He disposed of all offices and dignities; all rewards were received from his hands.

G------ had attained this vast influence at too early an age, and had risen by too rapid strides to enjoy his power with moderation. The eminence on which he beheld himself made his ambition dizzy, and no sooner was the final object of his wishes attained than his modesty forsook him. The respectful deference shown him by the first nobles of the land, by all who, in birth, fortune, and reputation, so far surpassed him, and which was even paid to him, youth as he was, by the oldest senators, intoxicated his pride, while his unlimited power served to develop a certain harshness which had been latent in his character, and which, throughout all the vicissitudes of his fortune, remained. There was no service, however considerable or toilsome, which his friends might not safely ask at his hands; but his enemies might well tremble! for, in proportion as he was extravagant in rewards, so was he implacable in revenge. He made less use of his influence to enrich himself than to render happy a number of beings who should pay homage to him as the author of their prosperity; but caprice alone, and not justice, dictated the choice of his subjects. By a haughty, imperious demeanor he alienated the hearts even of those whom he had most benefited; while at the same time he converted his rivals and secret enviers into deadly enemies.

Amongst those who watched all his movements with jealousy and envy, and who were silently preparing instruments for his destruction, was Joseph Martinengo, a Piedmontese count belonging to the prince's suite, whom G------ himself had formerly promoted, as an inoffensive creature, devoted to his interests, for the purpose of supplying his own place in attending upon the pleasures of the prince--an office which he began to find irksome, and which he willingly exchanged for more useful employment. Viewing this man merely as the work of his own hands, whom he might at any period consign to his former insignificance, he felt assured of the fidelity of his creature from motives of fear no less than of gratitude. He fell thus into the error committed by Richelieu, when he made over to Louis XII., as a sort of plaything, the young Le Grand. Without Richelieu's sagacity, however, to repair his error, he had to deal with a far more wily enemy than fell to the lot of the French minister.

Instead of boasting of his good fortune, or allowing his benefactor to feel that he could now dispense with his patronage, Martinengo was, on the contrary, the more cautious to maintain a show of dependence, and with studied humility affected to attach himself more and more closely to the author of his prosperity.

Meanwhile, he did not omit to avail himself, to its fullest extent, of the opportunities afforded him by his office, of being continually about the prince's person, to make himself daily more useful, and eventually indispensable to him. In a short time he had fathomed the prince's sentiments thoroughly, had discovered all the avenues to his confidence, and imperceptibly stolen himself into his favor. All those arts which a noble pride, and a natural elevation of character, had taught the minister to disdain, were brought into play by the Italian, who scrupled not to avail himself of the most despicable means for attaining his object. Well aware that man never stands so much in need of a guide and assistant as in the paths of vice, and that nothing gives a stronger title to bold familiarity than a participation in secret indiscretions, he took measures for exciting passions in the prince which had hitherto lain dormant, and then obtruded himself upon him as a confidant and an accomplice. He plunged him especially into those excesses which least of all endure witnesses, and imperceptibly accustomed the prince to make him the depository of secrets to which no third person was admitted. Upon the degradation of the prince's character he now began to found his infamous schemes of aggrandizement, and, as he had made secrecy a means of success, he had obtained entire possession of his master's heart before G------ even allowed himself to suspect that he shared it with another.

It may appear singular that so important a change should escape the minister's notice; but G------ was too well assured of his own worth ever to think of a man like Martinengo in the light of a competitor; while the latter was far too wily, and too much on his guard, to commit the least error which might tend to rouse his enemy from his fatal security. That which has caused thousands of his predecessors to stumble on the slippery path of royal favor was also the cause of G------'s fall, immoderate self-confidence. The secret intimacy between his creature, Martinengo, and his royal master gave him no uneasiness; he readily resigned a privilege which he despised and which had never been the object of his ambition. It was only because it smoothed his way to power that he had ever valued the prince's friendship, and he inconsiderately threw down the ladder by which he had risen as soon as he had attained the wished-for eminence.

Martinengo was not the man to rest satisfied with so subordinate a part. At each step which he advanced in the prince's favor his hopes rose higher, and his ambition began to grasp at a more substantial gratification. The deceitful humility which he had hitherto found it necessary to maintain towards his benefactor became daily more irksome to him, in proportion as the growth of his reputation awakened his pride. On the other hand, the minister's deportment toward him by no means improved with his marked progress in the prince's favor, but was often too visibly directed to rebuke his growing pride by reminding him of his humble origin. This forced and unnatural position having become quite insupportable, he at length formed the determination of putting an end to it by the destruction of his rival.

Under an impenetrable veil of dissimulation he brought his plan to maturity. He dared not venture as yet to come into open conflict with his rival; for, although the first glow of the minister's favor was at an end, it had commenced too early, and struck root too deeply in the bosom of the prince, to be torn from it abruptly. The slightest circumstance might restore it to all its former vigor; and therefore Martinengo well understood that the blow which he was about to strike must be a mortal one. Whatever ground G------ might have lost in the prince's affections he had gained in his respect. The more the prince withdrew himself from the affairs of state, the less could he dispense with the services of a man, who with the most conscientious devotion and fidelity had consulted his master's interests, even at the expense of the country,--and G------ was now as indispensable to him as a minister as he had formerly been dear to him as a friend.

By what means the Italian accomplished his purpose has remained a secret between those on whom the blow fell and those who directed it. It was reported that he laid before the prince the original draughts of a secret and very suspicious correspondence which G------ is said to have carried on with a neighboring court; but opinions differ as to whether the letters were authentic or spurious. Whatever degree of truth there may have been in the accusation it is but too certain that it fearfully accomplished the end in view. In the eyes of the prince G----- appeared the most ungrateful and vilest of traitors, whose treasonable practices were so thoroughly proved as to warrant the severest measures without further investigation. The whole affair was arranged with the most profound secrecy between Martinengo and his master, so that G------ had not the most distant presentiment of the impending storm. He continued wrapped in this fatal security until the dreadful moment in which he was destined, from being the object of universal homage and envy, to become that of the deepest commiseration.

When the decisive day arrived, G------ appeared, according to custom, upon the parade. He had risen in a few years from the rank of ensign to that of colonel; and even this was only a modest name for that of prime minister, which he virtually filled, and which placed him above the foremost of the land. The parade was the place where his pride was greeted with universal homage, and where he enjoyed for one short hour the dignity for which he endured a whole day of toil and privation. Those of the highest rank approached him with reverential deference, and those who were not assured of his favor with fear and trembling. Even the prince, whenever he visited the parade, saw himself neglected by the side of his vizier, inasmuch as it was far more dangerous to incur the displeasure of the latter than profitable to gain the friendship of the former. This very place, where he was wont to be adored as a god, had been selected for the dreadful theatre of his humiliation.

With a careless step he entered the well-known circle of courtiers, who, as unsuspicious as himself of what was to follow, paid their usual homage, awaiting his commands. After a short interval appeared Martinengo, accompanied by two adjutants, no longer the supple, cringing, smiling courtier, but overbearing and insolent, like a lackey suddenly raised to the rank of a gentleman. With insolence and effrontery he strutted up to the prime minister, and, confronting him with his head covered, demanded his sword in the prince's name. This was handed to him with a look of silent consternation; Martinengo, resting the naked point on the ground, snapped it in two with his foot, and threw the fragments at G-----'s feet. At this signal the two adjutants seized him; one tore the Order of the Cross from his breast; the other pulled off his epaulettes, the facings of his uniform, and even the badge and plume of feathers from his hat. During the whole of the appalling operation, which was conducted with incredible speed, not a sound nor a respiration was heard from more than five hundred persons who were present; but all, with blanched faces and palpitating hearts, stood in deathlike silence around the victim, who in his strange disarray--a rare spectacle of the melancholy and the ridiculous-- underwent a moment of agony which could only be equalled by feelings engendered on the scaffold. Thousands there are who in his situation would have been stretched senseless on the ground by the first shock; but his firm nerves and unflinching spirit sustained him through this bitter trial, and enabled him to drain the cup of bitterness to its dregs.

When this procedure was ended he was conducted through rows of thronging spectators to the extremity of the parade, where a covered carriage was in waiting. He was motioned to ascend, an escort of hussars being ready-mounted to attend to him. Meanwhile the report of this event had spread through the whole city; every window was flung open, every street lined with throngs of curious spectators, who pursued the carriage, shouting his name, amid cries of scorn and malicious exultation, or of commiseration more bitter to bear than either. At length he cleared the town, but here a no less fearful trial awaited him. The carriage turned out of the high road into a narrow, unfrequented path--a path which led to the gibbet, and alongside which, by command of the prince, he was borne at a slow pace. After he had suffered all the torture of anticipated execution the carriage turned off into the public road. Exposed to the sultry summer-heat, without refreshment or human consolation, he passed seven dreadful hours in journeying to the place of destination--a prison fortress. It was nightfall before he arrived; when, bereft of all consciousness, more dead than alive, his giant strength having at length yielded to twelve hours' fast and consuming thirst, he was dragged from the carriage; and, on regaining his senses, found himself in a horrible subterranean vault. The first object that presented itself to his gaze was a horrible dungeon-wall, feebly illuminated by a few rays of the moon, which forced their way through narrow crevices to a depth of nineteen fathoms. At his side he found a coarse loaf, a jug of water, and a bundle of straw for his couch. He endured this situation until noon the ensuing day, when an iron wicket in the centre of the tower was opened, and two hands were seen lowering a basket, containing food like that he had found the preceding night. For the first time since the terrible change in his fortunes did pain and suspense extort from him a question or two. Why was he brought hither? What offence had he committed? But he received no answer; the hands disappeared; and the sash was closed. Here, without beholding the face, or hearing the voice of a fellow-creature; without the least clue to his terrible destiny; fearful doubts and misgivings overhanging alike the past and the future; cheered by no rays of the sun, and soothed by no refreshing breeze; remote alike from human aid and human compassion; --here, in this frightful abode of misery, he numbered four hundred and ninety long and mournful days, which he counted by the wretched loaves that, day after day, with dreary monotony, were let down into his dungeon. But a discovery which he one day made early in his confinement filled up the measure of his affliction. He recognized the place. It was the same which he himself, in a fit of unworthy vengeance against a deserving officer, who had the misfortune to displease him, had ordered to be constructed only a few months before. With inventive cruelty he had even suggested the means by which the horrors of captivity might be aggravated; and it was but recently that he had made a journey hither in order personally to inspect the place and hasten its completion. What added the last bitter sting to his punishment was that the same officer for whom he had prepared the dungeon, an aged and meritorious colonel, had just succeeded the late commandant of the fortress, recently deceased, and, from having been the victim of his vengeance, had become the master of his fate. He was thus deprived of the last melancholy solace, the right of compassionating himself, and of accusing destiny, hardly as it might use him, of injustice. To the acuteness of his other suffering was now added a bitter self-contempt, contempt, and the pain which to a sensitive mind is the severest--dependence upon the generosity of a foe to whom he had shown none.

But that upright man was too noble-minded to take a mean revenge. It pained him deeply to enforce the severities which his instructions enjoined; but as an old soldier, accustomed to fulfil his orders to the letter with blind fidelity, he could do no more than pity, compassionate. The unhappy man found a more active assistant in the chaplain of the garrison, who, touched by the sufferings of the prisoner, which had just reached his ears, and then only through vague and confused reports, instantly took a firm resolution to do something to alleviate them. This excellent man, whose name I unwillingly suppress, believed he could in no way better fulfil his holy vocation than by bestowing his spiritual support and consolation upon a wretched being deprived of all other hopes of mercy.

As he could not obtain permission from the commandant himself to visit him he repaired in person to the capital, in order to urge his suit personally with the prince. He fell at his feet, and implored mercy for the unhappy man, who, shut out from the consolations of Christianity, a privilege from which even the greatest crime ought not to debar him, was pining in solitude, and perhaps on the brink of despair. With all the intrepidity and dignity which the conscious discharge of duty inspires, he entreated, nay demanded, free access to the prisoner, whom he claimed as a penitent for whose soul he was responsible to heaven. The good cause in which he spoke made him eloquent, and time had already somewhat softened the prince's anger. He granted him permission to visit the prisoner, and administer to his spiritual wants.

After a lapse of sixteen months, the first human face which the unhappy G------ beheld was that of his new benefactor. The only friend he had in the world he owed to his misfortunes, all his prosperity had gained him none. The good pastor's visit was like the appearance of an angel-- it would be impossible to describe his feelings, but from that day forth his tears flowed more kindly, for he had found one human being who sympathized with and compassionated him.

The pastor was filled with horror on entering the frightful vault. His eyes sought a human form, but beheld, creeping towards him from a corner opposite, which resembled rather the lair of a wild beast than the abode of anything human, a monster, the sight of which made his blood run cold. A ghastly deathlike skeleton, all the hue of life perished from a face on which grief and despair had traced deep furrows--his beard and nails, from long neglect, grown to a frightful length-his clothes rotten and hanging about him in tatters; and the air he breathed, for want of ventilation and cleansing, foul, fetid, and infectious. In this state be found the favorite of fortune;--his iron frame had stood proof against it all! Seized with horror at the sight, the pastor hurried back to the governor, in order to solicit a second indulgence for the poor wretch, without which the first would prove of no avail.

As the governor again excused himself by pleading the imperative nature of his instructions, the pastor nobly resolved on a second journey to the capital, again to supplicate the prince's mercy. There he protested solemnly that, without violating the sacred character of the sacrament, he could not administer it to the prisoner until some resemblance of the human form was restored to him. This prayer was also granted; and from that day forward the unfortunate man might be said to begin a new existence.

Several long years were spent by him in the fortress, but in a much more supportable condition, after the short summer of the new favorite's reign had passed, and others succeeded in his place, who either possessed more humanity or no motive for revenge. At length, after ten years of captivity, the hour of his delivery arrived, but without any judicial investigation or formal acquittal. He was presented with his freedom as a boon of mercy, and was, at the same time, ordered to quit his native country forever.

Here the oral traditions which I have been able to collect respecting his history begin to fail; and I find myself compelled to pass in silence over a period of about twenty years. During the interval G------ entered anew upon his military career, in a foreign service, which eventually brought him to a pitch of greatness quite equal to that from which he had, in his native country, been so awfully precipitated. At length time, that friend of the unfortunate, who works a slow but inevitable retribution, took into his hands the winding up of this affair. The prince's days of passion were over; humanity gradually resumed its sway over him as his hair whitened with age. At the brink of the grave he felt a yearning towards the friend of his early youth. In order to repay, as far as possible, the gray-headed old man, for the injuries which had been heaped upon the youth, the prince, with friendly expressions, invited the exile to revisit his native land, towards which for some time past G------'s heart had secretly yearned. The meeting was extremely trying, though apparently warm and cordial, as if they had only separated a few days before. The prince looked earnestly at his favorite, as if trying to recall features so well known to him, and yet so strange; he appeared as if numbering the deep furrows which he had himself so cruelly traced there. He looked searchingly in the old man's face for the beloved features of the youth, but found not what he sought. The welcome and the look of mutual confidence were evidently forced on both sides; shame on one side and dread on the other had forever separated their hearts. A sight which brought back to the prince's soul the full sense of his guilty precipitancy could not be gratifying to him, while G------ felt that he could no longer love the author of his misfortunes. Comforted, nevertheless, and in tranquillity, he looked back upon the past as the remembrance of a fearful dream.

In a short time G------ was reinstated in all his former dignities, and the prince smothered his feelings of secret repugnance by showering upon him the most splendid favors as some indemnification for the past. But could he also restore to him the heart which he had forever untuned for the enjoyment of life? Could he restore his years of hope? or make even a shadow of reparation to the stricken old man for what he had stolen from him in the days of his youth?

For nineteen years G------- continued to enjoy this clear, unruffled evening of his days. Neither misfortune nor age had been able to quench in him the fire of passion, nor wholly to obscure the genial humor of his character. In his seventieth year he was still in pursuit of the shadow of a happiness which he had actually possessed in his twentieth. He at length died governor of the fortress where state prisoners are confined. One would naturally have expected that towards these he would have exercised a humanity, the value of which he had been so thoroughly taught to appreciate in his own person; but he treated them with harshness and caprice; and a paroxysm of rage, in which he broke out against one of his prisoners, laid him in his coffin, in his eightieth year.

Printed in Great Britain
by Amazon